Anna Harvey
Y6

WHAT DO YOU THINK?

For Evie and Teddy
Let's agree, disagree and always be friends

First published in Great Britain in 2022 by Wren & Rook

ISBN: 978 1 5263 6493 7
E-book ISBN: 978 1 5263 6494 4

10 9 8 7 6 5 4 3 2 1

MIX
Paper from responsible sources
FSC® C104740

Wren & Rook
An imprint of
Hachette Children's Group
Part of Hodder & Stoughton
Carmelite House
50 Victoria Embankment
London EC4Y 0DZ

An Hachette UK Company
www.hachette.co.uk
www.hachettechildrens.co.uk

Printed in Italy.

WHAT DO YOU THINK?

HOW TO AGREE TO DISAGREE AND STILL BE FRIENDS

Matthew Syed

ILLUSTRATED BY
ASHWIN CHACKO

wren & rook

CONTENTS

INTRODUCTION

WHAT DO YOU THINK?

NOW THERE'S A QUESTION

THAT NO ONE ASKS VERY OFTEN

RIGHT?

Like, no one asked me what I thought when my dad bought a bulk load of onions (half price because they were past their best), started cutting them all in half and put them in every single corner of the house. Including the loft.

I thought that this new idea of his wasn't going to end well.

And it didn't.

BUT NO ONE ASKED ME.

One onion accidentally ended up in the washing machine and I had to wear a school uniform that smelt like a kebab shop all week. And, as I would have predicted, my dad totally forgot about the ones in the loft. And after a small heatwave, the ones up there were not just past their best, they were past their worst and full of maggots. Which rapidly turned to massive flies. And when he went up there to investigate the buzzing, he entered a cloud of flies head first and swallowed at least three, he thinks.

If he'd asked me, I would have told him it was a bad idea. But he didn't. And the Syed family haven't eaten an onion since.

But . . . why on earth was he putting onions everywhere?

WHAT **WAS** HE THINKING?

Who knows . . . but let's come back to that in a minute. I am feeling a bit sick from thinking about the fly-swallowing right now.

If you are anything like me (and I don't mean bald and into wearing tracksuits), then I bet you are thinking lots of thoughts all of the time. And you've got opinions about things. And ideas. And good ones too. About all kinds of things.

My mind is sometimes fizzing with so many thoughts that I wonder where they all come from.

I'm sure some of them probably just come from being hungry. Because I think about burgers and ice cream quite a lot.

But what about the others? The thoughts about what is going on at school? At home? About what to spend my birthday money on? About the planet warming up faster than my dad doing a Joe Wicks session (believe me, he reaches about a hundred degrees after thirty seconds)? About children going hungry? About what's happening in the news?

WHICH GOT ME
THINKING (HMMM . . .
EVEN MORE THOUGHTS!!)

Why do we think like we do?

And are we always right?

And what do we do if it turns out we are wrong after all?

Being in control of what we think is important. Knowing our mind helps us to recognise and communicate not just what we believe, but how we are feeling too.

So, how do we let other people know what we think, without ending up in a big row, storming off and saying something we'll probably regret later?

I didn't speak to my brother for two weeks once because he didn't agree about who I thought was the best striker for the England football team. It went something like this:

Nice chat for about ten minutes, talking about different tactics, matches and great goals.
ME AND HIM
You're just wrong, though. You haven't even looked at the stats.
HIM
YES, I HAVE. And what do you know? You are rubbish at football anyway. You've scored so many own goals this season, Coach Tom wants to pick you for the opposition.
ME (getting annoyed)
SHUT UP. AND GET YOUR MASSIVE NOSE OUT OF MY FACE.
HIM (getting even more annoyed)

NIGHTMARE.

We went from best friends to arch-enemies in the space of ten minutes and thirty seconds. And I still worry about the size of my nose every time I look in the mirror.

And all because we had a slight difference of opinion. About a game. Which we both love.

And this doesn't just happen to us. It happens everywhere – in schools, in families, amongst friends, in offices, on social media, on TV and even with the Prime Minister and the people who don't agree with them. Everywhere.

People getting into major fights over ideas they should be able to disagree about and talk through, then shake hands and carry on being friends. Even if they still disagree.

So you can see, it **REALLY** is a complicated business . . . all this thinking and agreeing and disagreeing.

And the problems don't end there . . .

You can't even be sure that everything you see, read or hear is true. Because there are actually people out there happy to publish news and information that is just false – to confuse us, to make us believe in the wrong things and to form our thoughts based on faulty facts.

WHO would do that? WHY would anyone do that?
I don't know. BUT . . .

FAKE NEWS IS REAL.

Confused? Me too.

So . . . don't be hard on yourself if you find you want to change your mind. It can be really difficult to sift through all of the things we are told and be able to decide what WE think.

And even when we have waded through the maze of misinformation out there and decided what we really think, talking about it with our friends and family can be as dangerous as starting World War Three. But that is what this book is for.

To help us understand exactly how we think. How we are influenced. How we make our decisions. How we talk about them without getting into an argument. And how we can change our mind (if we need to).

Back to my dad and the onions . . .

It was a bad case of FAKE NEWS. My dad had read somewhere that peeled onions absorb germs and bacteria. So my dad (and thousands of other people) thought that if you scattered them around your house like confetti, they would pick up all the bad stuff in the air and you'd never catch a cold, flu or coronavirus again.

Awesome, he thought. These slightly see-through vegetables might be the answer to a long and healthy life for the Syed family. And living with a bunch of rotting onions in your living room is surely a small price to pay if it means we would all live to 103.

That was his thinking.

Except his thinking was wrong. Because they don't absorb any bacteria at all. There is no scientific evidence of any health benefits of chucking raw onion randomly round your loft. Even the National Association of Onions (yes, that really is a thing) came out and said so.

And if this can happen to my dad (an actual university professor) . . . this can happen to anyone.

So . . . we had better get on with this book . . . before we start putting courgettes in our school bag because someone said they make your PE kit less stinky.

They don't, by the way . . .

CHAPTER 1
ARE YOU A JUMPER?

Mr Phelan was a jumper.

A MASSIVE JUMPER.

And I don't mean the kind of jumper that your mum makes you wear when it isn't even cold. Or the kind of jumper that wins a gold medal at the Olympics in the 'who can transport their bottom the furthest distance before landing it into a massive sand pit' competition.

No. Mr Phelan (our new teacher) was a massive jumper. Of a different kind. Let me explain . . .

Mr Phelan arrived new to our school at the start of term in a yellow car with its roof down.

He wasn't like any of our other teachers. Or really like anyone I had ever met. He wore bright gold sunglasses to assembly on the first day. I mean . . .

And he didn't seem to know what he was doing when we got to the classroom. He made all the boys sit on one side of the room and all the girls on the other. 'I assume you all hate each other at this age,' he said.

I am not sure why he thought that. And it meant I was miles away from Emma, who was one of my best friends.

My dad loved Mr Phelan to start with. He said he was good at making decisions. That he was a 'quick thinker' and just what the school needed. He even called him Decisive Derek after he put me in the top maths group on the first day of term.

His name wasn't Derek. It was Eric. But details like that didn't seem to concern my dad too much. Anyway . . .

All was going well for a while. I got on to the football team. It was before we'd even played, which was a bit odd, but I was happy.

'Decisive Derek can see your potential,' said my dad, ignoring the fact that Mr Phelan was yet to even see me kick a ball. But then it all went sideways.

And Decisive Derek (Eric) fell out of my dad's good books. In quite spectacular fashion. And this is when we realised just how big a jumper (no, not that kind of jumper) Mr Phelan was.

He'd decided we should have a class cooking competition. This had never happened before. It was a bit daunting because he seemed to think we would all be great chefs. But far as I knew, we weren't. Mark had once managed a bean on toast (he dropped the tin and all but one bean fell on the floor). And I had managed to almost burn down the local bakery in search of a croissant for breakfast (that's another story, though).

But Decisive Derek was pressing ahead with this idea. And it was going to be a competition. And everyone was getting increasingly worried.

And then it happened. The day before the cook off, Mr Phelan asked us to tell him what we planned to make. But before we had time to speak, he piled in with . . .

Don't tell me. Emma, I know you'll be thinking of some pretty pink cupcakes. And Matthew, I am looking forward to tasting your curry.

SORRY. WHAT? CURRY?

Why on earth would he think I was going to make that? I couldn't understand it. I was going to do a cheese pizza.

And why would he think Emma would make pretty pink cupcakes? She hated pink. Her favourite colour was blue; she supported Manchester City.

But Mr Phelan had JUMPED . . . as usual . . .

TO A **MASSIVE** CONCLUSION.

He thought that Emma would be keen on fluffy pink cupcakes because she was a girl.

WRONG!

And he thought that I would be making a curry because my dad was from Pakistan and we must eat curry all of the time at home.

WRONG AGAIN!

He CLEARLY did not know my dad at all. And when I mentioned all this to my dad, Mr Phelan quickly was demoted from being Decisive Derek to Doofus Derek. My dad paid him a swift visit and explained, with the use of a picture of our Christmas dinner (where my grandad was asleep at the table), that IN FACT a roast was his favourite meal.

It went from bad to worse. Rather than apologising for his mistaken assumptions on the curry, Mr Phelan asked my dad whether he realised that my grandad had died at the dinner table on Christmas day.

HE'S ASLEEP, YOU FOOL

shouted my dad. 'Why would you assume he was dead! Do you think we wouldn't have noticed!' And he stormed out of the school.

Things unravelled for Mr Phelan pretty quickly after that. He had no idea what he was doing. It turned out that this was one in a long line of conclusions he had jumped to:

- *The top maths groups* – he had put me in there because he thought my head was big! He hadn't taught maths before, apparently, but had *assumed* that you'd need a big brain to be good at it, and big brains would mean a big head. My head wasn't even that big; I just had a lot of hair (yes, I know I have none now), but he hadn't accounted for that.

- *The football team* – he had picked it based on SHOE SIZE. He *assumed* that massive feet meant more goals. Which it doesn't, by the way; Cristiano Ronaldo has small feet and he's not bad.

- *The whole 'career' in teaching thing* – it was a new career for him. He used to organise parties in Spain (which explained the car and the sunglasses) and thought that teaching would be basically the same thing. You know . . . crowds of people to organise and long summer holidays. It turned out to be really quite different.

Mr Phelan lasted until half term. He headed off on a one-way ticket to Barcelona and back to his party planning.

You are probably wondering where on earth all this is going. You might be thinking this is totally irrelevant to the book you thought you were reading.

BUT . . . let's not jump to conclusions (see what I did there?) because in fact, Mr Phelan's behaviour and way of thinking tells us quite a bit about how we make decisions and how easy it is to form opinions that are not quite right.

So, are you ready for a bit of

NEUROSCIENCE?

Don't groan . . . I promise it will be fun (even when we get to the maths question. I'm not even joking).

First take a really quick look at this picture . . .

What were your first thoughts? I'm guessing that you saw that this is a girl, probably a teenager, definitely with dark hair. But I am also guessing that you thought she looked annoyed, that she was about to shout something loud and angry at someone (maybe she has just found out about the fake onion news? My dad looked a bit like this when he was clearing the onions out of the loft . . .).

Very quickly your brain made some assumptions about this girl in the picture and what she was thinking and feeling. And this entered your head automatically. Without thinking. Am I right?

Well . . . (and here is the science) a guy called Daniel Kahneman certainly thinks so. He is a professor at Princeton University in America and a seriously smart guy. He has even won a Nobel Prize. And he has done some very interesting work on how we think and why we make decisions.

He believes that we all have two ways of thinking. Fast Thinking and Slow Thinking.

Fast Thinking is what happened when you looked at that picture. Without even trying, you made assumptions and formed opinions about the girl. The same way you might do if your best friend was crying . . . you'd automatically think they were sad or unhappy. And this is the same Fast Thinking that might make you jump out of the way of a speeding car or scream at a big juicy spider in the bath (or is that just me?).

Fast Thinking is usually brilliant (unless you are Mr Phelan, but we'll come back to that guy in a minute). It helps us take stock of situations quickly and react to keep ourselves safe. Imagine if you took five minutes to move away from that spider? Its hairy legs might be on your neck by then . . . **EWWWWWW.**

Now, like the picture before, take a quick look at these letters . . .

C E N L O I S

Spot any words?

Maybe you did. But I am guessing you didn't.

You probably did have some fast thoughts, though. Ones that just happened. I suspect you recognised these as letters from the alphabet? And you knew that they are capital letters and written in black ink?

But if I asked you to rearrange them to make a five-letter word, like you might do if these were your stash of letters in Scrabble . . . well . . . that is a bit too much for your fast-thinking abilities. You'd need to stop and think about it. Try a few options maybe . . .

CLINE . . . no

INLOC . . . no

COLIN . . . yep, he is there. Anyone know a Colin?

Eventually you might work out that **NOISE** is there. So is **SLICE**. So is **CLONE**.

Now . . . what was happening when you were decoding and analysing the letters is what Daniel Kahneman calls Slow Thinking.

It isn't automatic like Fast Thinking. You needed to remember your spellings from Year 1. You needed to rearrange the letters and hold those in your head while you racked your brains for five-letter words that would score you more points than Colin.

It takes effort and time to work this out. It is slower. And Slow Thinking is brilliant for making good decisions. It forces us to consider what we are being asked and think through what we already know – and how we feel – before we make a decision.

Both Fast Thinking and Slow Thinking are super important.

RECAP: Fast Thinking just happens; thoughts and instincts pop into our mind without us having to do any work.

Like how I know exactly what my mum is thinking by the way she says my name. If it is shouty and spikey – 'MA . . . TTHEW!!!!' – then I just know she has found the twelve pairs of dirty socks under my bed. Now, on the other hand, with Slow Thinking we have to put the time in, make calculations, make choices, decide on things. It is considered. Thoughtful.

Like if I decide to calculate 23 x 17. I don't know my 17 times tables (do you? Thought not), and so I have to spend the time to work it out. Or like when I write an article for the newspaper. I have to spend time deciding what I think. And then thinking about the best order to write those thoughts down. It doesn't just happen.

So . . . we now know about the two types of thinking we have. *FAST THINKING* and S L O W THINKING. An awesome pairing. Brilliant brain wiring. Working in harmony to help us react, decide and act in the best way possible. Operating a little bit like Harry and Hermione. Harry puts up a fight if he can, but needs to hand over to Hermione if there is any serious thinking or working out to be done in the library.

Right? Perfect . . . Except when it isn't . . .

You see . . . while this system is often brilliant, sometimes it lets us down.

Take a look at these lines:

WHICH ONE DO YOU THINK IS LONGER?

I KNOW YOU'VE GOT AN ANSWER ALREADY.

You reckon the top one is longer.

I AM RIGHT, AREN'T I?

Now, your Fast Thinking piled in . . . and made that assumption for you. But, if you had used some Slow Thinking and gone and got a ruler and measured the lines, you would know that the lines are actually the exact same length (go on, try it).

And this is an example of where our Fast Thinking jumps to an answer too quickly. We make a decision or form an opinion that isn't quite right. And unless we bring in our Slow Thinking and actually 'go and get the ruler', we might end up betting all of our pocket money on the wrong answer.

But often we don't take the time to think slowly. We bust in with our assumptions.

This takes us back to Mr Phelan. And why he thought that I would be cooking a curry in the school *MasterChef* (or Disaster Chef, as Emma was calling it) competition. You see, he had allowed his Fast Thinking to take one look at my skin colour and assume I must love curry because my dad is from Pakistan.

If he had done any Slow Thinking, talked to me for three minutes for example, I could have told him that my dad had lived in Reading for twelve years, and although he could probably eat a chilli faster than most people, what he actually loved the most was roast chicken, followed closely by a deep-pan margherita.

Mr Phelan had jumped to a conclusion without using his Slow Thinking. He had done the same with Emma and the pink cupcakes. The big feet and the football team. Even the top maths group and the big head thing.

When Mr Phelan left after just half a term that was the last we ever saw of him, it had got me thinking . . .

Do we all do this? Do we all jump to conclusions? Using our Fast Thinking without taking the time to let our Slow Thinking kick in and analyse what is really going on?

I am coming to the (Slow Thinking) conclusion that we might do. And it might mean that some of the thoughts we have and opinions we form might not reflect what we would think or feel if we had given ourselves more time to consider things.

SLOW DOWN

So, while you might have thought that you were totally in control of your decisions and opinions, this chapter has shown that we can all think too fast sometimes. But don't worry, because this book is going to show you how to slow down your thinking. How to understand the things that are influencing you and how to take the time to analyse all of the information around you. And this is going to help you make better decisions that you can feel confident in.

AWESOME.

LET'S GET INTO IT . . .

CHAPTER 2

BAD INFLUENCE

It isn't every day that you come home and find your mum and dad sitting in the front garden. In the rain. On a mustard-yellow leather sofa. Feet up on the matching mustard-yellow pouffe. With Barry from next door sitting in between them. But that was exactly what was going on.

I had been to table tennis practice and I was a bit late because me and Jimmy Stokes had taken one of our Big Mac Meal detours on the way back. I was worried that this welcoming committee in the garden had rumbled me and I was about to get in to trouble for ruining my dinner.

'What's going on?' I asked while nervously checking that I hadn't left any burger or ketchup evidence on my chin.

'Don't you just love it?' shouted my dad as he started to show me the sofa's remote-controlled footrests. 'The colour is unbelievable, it's PURE GOLD.' That was debatable. It looked more like that American-style cheese that you can spray from a can.

At this point my mum looked as if she was going to burst. With rage or into tears, I couldn't tell. But she was furious. And I realised that Barry from next door wasn't sitting in the middle for his own enjoyment; he was acting as a peacekeeper to stop my mum from potentially killing my dad.

'Errr . . . Did we need a new sofa?' I asked tentatively. The old one we had seemed perfectly fine to me. And was exactly the same as the new one, apart from the colour.

NO!

OH YES.
EVERYONE NEEDS A SOFA LIKE THIS

came the simultaneous shouts from my mum and my dad.

Barry was looking very nervous now.

I wasn't sure whether to risk another question. But decided I might as well.

'And . . . errr . . . why is it out here in the garden?'

At this, Barry got up and went home. He'd had enough and knew that he wasn't going to be able to keep my mum calm for very much longer.

BECAUSE YOUR DAD IS A TOTAL FOOL

and she stormed off, leaving my dad caressing the mustard-yellow headrest.

WHO'S IN CONTROL?

On one level, this is a silly story about a weird-looking leather sofa. But on another, it explains a lot about how our decision-making and thinking happens. And how we might feel like we are in control of our choices when in fact there are usually other influences at play.

We know from chapter 1 that we can jump to conclusions. That our own brain can think too fast and we can end up with answers, assumptions and opinions that don't quite reflect what we really think or feel. But what if there are *other* influences out there? Things capable of persuading us to think in a certain way? Influences that cause us to jump to those conclusions. Or even worse . . . guide us to views and opinions (and sofas, as it turns out) that might actually be wrong.

And what if we don't even notice that this is happening?

So . . . wait . . . let's get this straight because this is sounding like bad news. We might not be in control of what we think?

OMG . . . this is sounding like there might be aliens out there controlling our brains. Has there been an alien invasion and no one has noticed?

Because mind control would definitely explain that mustard-coloured sofa.

But . . . no . . . of course there hasn't. Our thoughts aren't being controlled by aliens. But we ARE easily influenced, and we've seen how we can jump to the wrong conclusions without meaning to, thanks to Fast Thinking.

So, to stop us from buying sofas we don't need, copying our friends without thinking or blindly believing what we see on YouTube, it is worth being aware of HOW we can be influenced. Because . . . if we are aware of WHY we think the way we do, then we can be more in control of our thoughts and opinions and make better decisions for ourselves.

Now let's get into this, and quick. One of our biggest INFLUENCERS is right in front of us, and it is important that we know about it. And, no I don't mean that guy off YouTube with 1,300,900 followers . . . I mean all of the small, sneaky tricks out there that can send our Fast Thinking into overdrive.

PRICEY DOGS

Would you spend £55 on a hot dog?

'HOW MUCH?' I hear you cry.

Let's not go into the detail of what is in an actual hot dog right now, but £55 seems like way too much money for a bread roll and some bits of a pig squished together with some ketchup. Now, we can't be sure of which bits (sorry, I know I said I wouldn't go there), but we can be fairly sure it is not the expensive pig bits and even if it were, the hot dog still wouldn't be worth £55.

But a New York restaurant was charging exactly that: £55 for their 'haute dog' – a fancy name for what they said was the most expensive hot dog in the world. Unsurprisingly they didn't sell many. But guess what? Sales of their £14.50 hamburger and fries, which had been pretty slow, rocketed when they put the mega-pricey dog on the menu.

I mean, £14.50 is still quite a lot for a cow patty (calm down . . . I said patty) between two hunks of a loaf. Even if the fries are thrown in. But, nevertheless, these burgers started flying off of the grill like never before.

But why? What was going on?

You see, £55 acts as something that scientists call an Anchor. Despite the fact that even Jeff Bezos (you know, founded Amazon, has like £110 billion in the bank) would NEVER pay as much as £55 for a sausage, that price gets stuck in our mind. Like a heavy anchor, it starts weighing our thoughts down, and we can't seem to forget about it. And it begins to influence how we think.

So when we see **£14.50** for a beefburger on the same menu, we think it is cheap. A bargain, we cheer. And whip out our wallets in wild celebration. We can't part with our money fast enough, desperate to get our chops round that meaty deal of the century.

But we have lost our minds. We could go down the road to McDonald's and buy a Big Mac Meal for under £4 (I should know . . . I've just been down there and had two – **DO NOT** tell my mum).

But instead of comparing the price of our meal to what we might pay for it if we went to a different restaurant, which would make sense if we used our Slow Thinking, we don't. We jump right in with our Fast

Thinking and start comparing it to some totally irrelevant dish that we'd NEVER buy. And neither would anyone else.

And here is the thing . . . shops and advertisers use Anchors as a way of influencing us to buy all kinds of things that we might not even need or be able to afford.

Now . . . you might be beginning to see the link with the spray-on-cheese-coloured sofa in our garden. But more on this later . . .

ANCHOR ALERT!

Are you seeing 99p everywhere you go? Well, that is no surprise. When you see a price of £5.99 in a shop, they are using an Anchor to try and influence you. Hoping you'll think it isn't really much more than £5. A bargain! It isn't really and will leave you with a ton of pennies weighing down your pockets. But it works, and items priced at 99p or £5.99 sell more than if they were priced at £1 or £6.

But this type of influence affects much more than prices and shopping. And we definitely want to be aware of the other ways we might jump to conclusions.

Here is another example. Have you heard of Mahatma Gandhi? It doesn't really matter if you haven't, but he was a famous lawyer who campaigned peacefully for India's independence from British rule. Anyway, a group of people were asked to guess what age Gandhi was when he died.

But before they were asked for their estimate, the group was split into two and they were asked a slightly different question.

The first group was asked, 'Did Gandhi die before or after the age of nine?'

The other group was asked, 'Did Gandhi die before or after the age of one hundred and forty?'

Now, the first group obviously must have been aware that Gandhi was older than nine when he died. I mean, he was a massively famous lawyer. How many of those do you know who are only eight years old?

Equally, the second group knew that he couldn't have been older than one hundred and forty when he died. The oldest person to ever live has so far only made it to one hundred and twenty-two years old. So the answer was obviously less than that.

But adding in this small extra question about Gandhi's possible age when he died had some very interesting effects. It anchored each group and influenced their answer to the question.

The group who were asked whether he died before or after he was nine years old applied some Fast Thinking. They jumped to the conclusion that Gandhi must have been very young when he died. 'Why else would they mention him being nine years old?' they thought.

And the other group thought that this guy must have lived for ages. 'Why else would they mention him being one hundred and forty years old?' they thought.

But the anchors of nine and one hundred and forty years old were much like the price of £55 for the hot dog. Totally irrelevant. Not related to the actual answer at all. Which, by the way, is seventy-eight years old.

But the group with the lower anchor (age nine) guessed Gandhi was just fifty when he died. And the group with the higher anchor (age one hundred and forty) guessed he was sixty-seven.

Getting people to think about a random number before you ask them a question can really influence the conclusions they come to.

'Now, what on earth does all this mean for me?' I hear you asking. Or maybe you are not asking that and are still thinking about how expensive that £55 hot dog was.

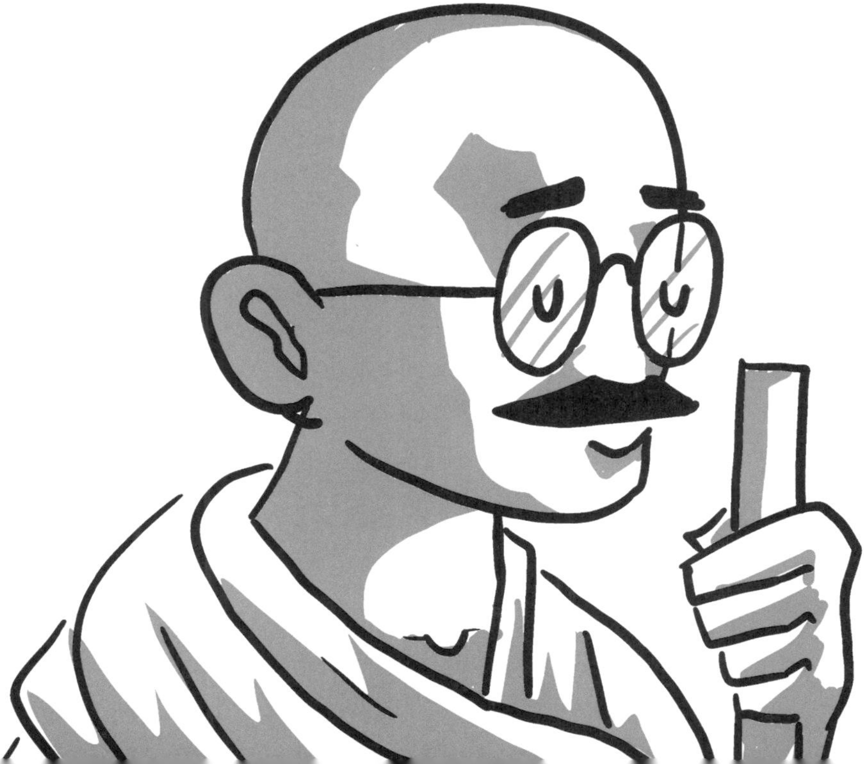

Well, for my dad it meant that he bought a sofa he didn't need. He spent the money my mum had been saving for a holiday on a bright yellow leather three-seater chair and matching pouffe that didn't even fit through the front door. He had only gone out to buy a tin of spaghetti hoops for lunch. But on the way he had driven past the furniture shop with a sign saying 'Final clearance sale', and he couldn't resist. My dad LOVES a bargain.

When he got in there, they had a very stylish black sofa for sale at full price for £9,000. The same sofa in the less stylish 'spray-on cheese' colour was only £1,999 (those pesky 99s again!). And that was it. My dad fell hook, line and anchor (see what I did there?) for the tactics. He thought he had found the deal of his lifetime and bundled it on to the roof-rack of the car with the speed and precision of a Formula 1 team doing a mid-race pit stop.

It wasn't until he got home that he realised it was wider than our front door. (Why spend time measuring up when the world's biggest bargain is in front of you?) Or that Barry had seen the same sofa in the Argos catalogue for only £1,500 the previous week. Or that our current sofa was just fine. And fitted inside the house.

Just like my dad, we have a tendency to take the **first bit** of information we have been told or that we come across (like the price of the hot dog, the nicer sofa or Gandhi's age when he died) and use our Fast Thinking to base all our judgements on that. It means that we can end up saying things, making decisions or acting in a way that we don't mean to.

QUESTIONS AND ANCHORS

We have seen that the way questions are asked can significantly influence the way we think and respond. Here is another example . . .

Environmental Impact

A local council were trying to reduce the number of cars driving through the parks in the area. So they sent out a survey to ask residents their opinion. The first question they asked was a bit like this:

'Would you like cleaner air and less pollution in your parks?'

And guess what . . . almost everyone said YES! Who wouldn't want that?

What they didn't ask was:

'Would you like us to close the roads in the parks so cars are no longer permitted?'

Of course, this is how they planned to make the air cleaner. But it would also result in people's journey times home from work or school being much longer as the surrounding roads struggled to cope with the extra traffic that used to travel through the park.

Based on their survey question, the council closed the park to traffic. And not everyone was happy that they hadn't been asked a more balanced question.

JUST LIKE ME? MAYBE NOT . . .

In our house we LOVED *Star Wars*. All of it. I saw (well, still see) myself as Hans Solo flying the *Millennium Falcon*. And as my brother got hairier, he was a very good stand-in for Chewbacca.

So I couldn't believe it when my best friend Mark said it was a rubbish film.

He said he preferred . . . *Ghostbusters*.

I mean. WHAT? A film starring a bright green blob called Slimer was better than *Star Wars*?

How could he be my best friend and think that? I didn't speak to him for a whole maths lesson.

But it's (very) possible I was unknowingly influenced by my own family and their preferences. And it is (very) possible that you might be too. When I think about it, I'd only seen *Ghostbusters* once and I was trying to do my geography homework at the same time, so I wasn't really concentrating. Plus my mum came in and turned it off halfway through because she is scared of ghosts ever since my friend Mark came to our Halloween party as a reasonably realistic headless horseman. Anyway, the point is that I don't even know how *Ghostbusters* ends. Hmmm . . . maybe I need to give it another go before I definitely decide *Star Wars* is better . . .

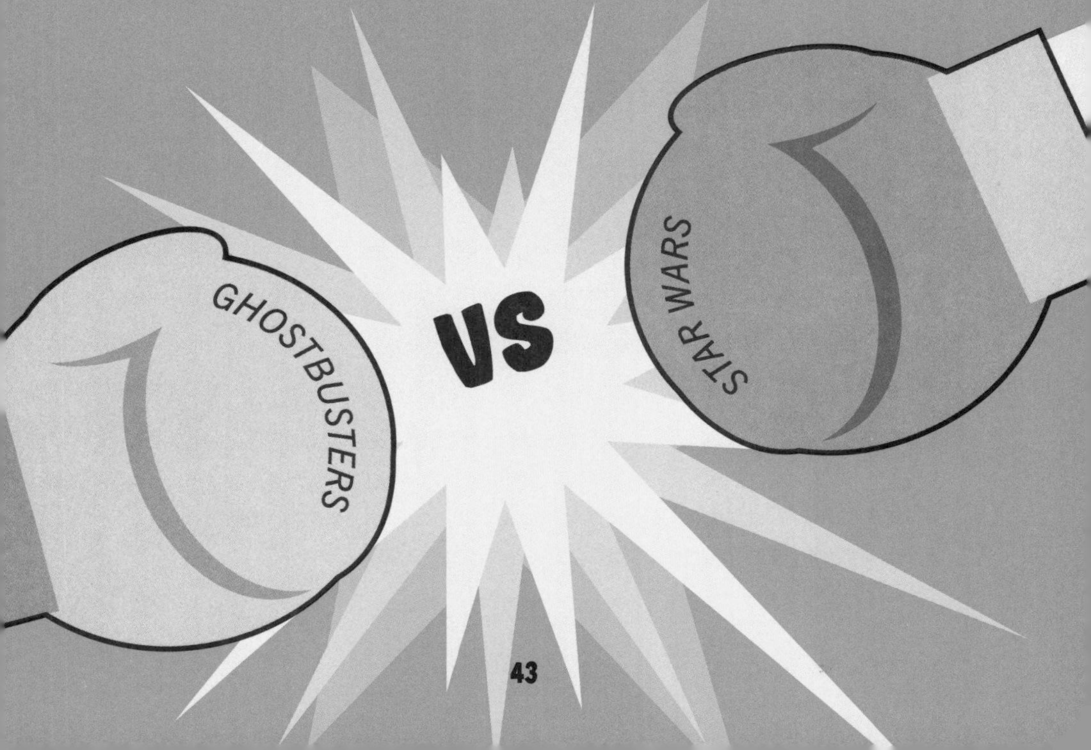

To add to how confusing influences can be, we often assume that other families are just like ours. That they like the same things and act and think in the same way as we do.

This can mean that we expect other people to like the same stuff as us and agree with our opinions (why wouldn't they if they are just like we are?) when in fact they might not.

Because every family is different. And quite possibly VERY different because their influences are different.

They might:

- BELIEVE IN A DIFFERENT RELIGION
- HAVE DIFFERENT THOUGHTS ON POLITICS
- SUPPORT A DIFFERENT FOOTBALL TEAM
- GO TO BED AT A DIFFERENT TIME
- EAT DIFFERENT FOOD FOR BREAKFAST
- WEAR CLOTHES THAT ARE NOTHING LIKE YOURS

Given all of the things that could be different, don't be surprised if they have different opinions and you disagree sometimes.

TEACHER TROUBLE

But influence doesn't just affect what we buy, how we behave or even the arguments we can get into. It can impact how people behave towards US. Like at school. Imagine your new teacher reads your report from last year. It says you were a bit naughty, didn't focus enough in your science lessons. And that's it, she is anchored. She thinks you're worse than a cross between Horrid Henry and Draco Malfoy. And that opinion has stuck. You can't seem to shift her. Even though you have turned over a brand-new leaf this year and are student of the century, she still thinks you are planning to set fire to the classroom with the Bunsen burner when she turns her back.

This also reminds me a bit of Mr Phelan. Jumping to conclusions about my curry-making skills, just because of my skin colour. Sadly this kind of thing happens often. And can be upsetting if someone has been influenced to think something about you that isn't right.

WHAT'S UP, DOC?

Your doctor might do it too. You have been complaining of a tummy ache the last few times you've been to see her. She decides it is an allergy to eating wheat. She's right. So no more doughnuts for you! But when you go back next time with a tummy pain, she is anchored to her previous diagnosis. She thinks you've been back on the Krispy Kremes and doesn't take enough notice when you tell her the pain doesn't feel the same, and it isn't in the same place. The next thing you know, you're having your appendix (that small tube attached to your intestine) removed in hospital. All because your doctor was too influenced by her previous diagnosis to spot it.

So don't be afraid to respectfully question the decisions that other people make if they affect you, even if those people seem really important, like doctors or teachers. Ask how they came up with their view. And probe to find out whether there are any anchoring influences going on.

SOCIAL MEDIA

Whether you're already an influencer racking up a following as big as Cristiano Ronaldo's or not on social media yet, we're all still influenced by social media every day. (Spoiler Alert: you have to be over thirteen to sign up to most social media platforms – it's a rule that's there to protect you because, as you'll soon see, you really do have to be careful online.) From TikTok challenges causing mayhem in the playground to having arguments about fake news, there's no escaping it. So no matter if you love it, hate it or just don't see the point, it's good to arm yourself against the ways social media can impact your life.

Did you know ... it is estimated that 4.62 billion people are on social media. And the average person spends nearly two and half hours a day looking at it. Wowsers. That is a lot of time. If you add that up, it is the same as 140 school days! Every year. Just staring at a phone checking in on cute iguana pictures or Kim Kardashian's new hair colour.

But it also means that social media is a mega place to try to influence billions of people every day. Not all of these influences are good ones, though.

Some of the time, social media is a useful place, to buy stuff, connect with people or read the news and find out what is happening all over the world.

But sometimes there are problems. Because it is also a place where not everyone is totally honest. And so we can be influenced to like or buy things that might not be as good as they seem.

I bought a shirt once. The guy in the picture looked amazing wearing it. He was on a beach, wearing his dark green cotton shirt, silver buttons, one hand on a palm tree. He looked seriously cool (at least I thought so anyway) and I wanted to look like him. But I didn't. Because when it arrived, it was NOTHING LIKE the picture. It was completely see-through, three sizes too big ... and the colour of a tennis ball. I looked like I was wearing a tent that the emergency services might use.

People also post fake news on social media (we'll come back to that later). And, worryingly, lots of people filter their photos, alter the way they look and present their life in a way that doesn't entirely reflect reality. They are hoping to influence others with their exciting escapades so they edit out the bad bits and only show the good bits.

This can sometimes make people feel a bit down. If we compare their life to ours . . . maybe ours isn't quite as exciting. Maybe we aren't quite as cool as they are. Maybe we don't look as good as they do. And maybe we aren't as popular and we wouldn't get as many followers as they have.

But, remember the tennis-ball-green shirt? It was NOTHING LIKE the pictures. And that is so often the case with the content we see online. It just doesn't reflect real life.

So, don't let yourself fall for these influences. Don't let anything you see online dent your confidence. You are awesome and if you know your own mind (this book will help you with that) then you can decide what you think for yourself.

P.S. Did you know . . . you can even buy followers on social media. £10.99 for 1,000 last time I looked. So their followers might not even be real!

UNDO THE INFLUENCE

Because these influences – anchors, friends, family, the internet – often happen to us without us even realising, it can be hard to break free of them. A good way to at least try to be in control of our thoughts and opinions is to think about alternative points of view. Sometimes doing this might even change what we think.

Like 'What if we just don't buy a sofa the in the same colour as the IKEA logo after all?' or 'Should I watch *Ghostbusters* again before I tell Mark that he is the world's biggest loser?'

Taking the time to do this would at least give your Slow Thinking some space to work its magic. And even if you don't change your mind, you will feel more in control of the decision you have made.

TOP TIP:

PS . . . Shhhhh . . . You could use this whole anchoring business to your advantage. To help you in your own negotiations.

Parents, stop reading right now. You might not like what I am about to say . . .

So, for example, next time you want more time on your phone/console/maths homework (I threw that last one in just in case any parents are still reading!), use some anchoring and see if it helps.

Imagine you are hoping for an extra hour a day. Ask for an extra five hours a day. They'll scream. They'll shout and tell you this is crazy talk (which it is). Then you say you'll compromise with a just an hour a day. And I bet you they jump at the chance of a mere sixty minutes, thinking that this is hardly any extra time at all after you've anchored them at five hours. Genius . . .

CHAPTER 3

FAKE NEWS, MY FRIEND

Sofa update: It went back to the shop. My dad got a quote to widen the doorway so that it would fit into the house. It was going to be £900. Which suddenly made his bargain seem less like the deal of the decade. And more like a major hassle.

So . . . my mum took it back for the refund. She didn't trust my dad. Not only did she think he would decide to keep the sofa and bring it back home, but she was worried he might take a fancy to the velvet king-size bed which was now in the shop window sporting the words 'Cut price' across the headboard.

For a while things went back to normal. Well, as normal as things ever got in the Syed household. Until one Sunday morning . . .

My dad was doing his skipping exercises. He had to do 3,000 every day to keep himself 'trim' (his words). But, here's the thing, he refused to buy a skipping rope.

Now, to anyone else, this would be totally weird. But to my dad, this was just good financial sense. Why purchase a skipping rope when (in his view) it was totally unnecessary. Why waste £7.99 when you could just jump over thin air? All while flailing your wrists around like windmills, pretending you were skipping.

And while all his puffing and panting was happening in the living room, my mum was wallpapering their bedroom. And my mum likes a bold wallpaper. No sweet flowers or hexagonal patterns for her. No chance. And this latest project (in a long line of DIY projects) was possibly her boldest yet. It was a full-on beach scene from somewhere in Miami. It was meant to make her feel like she was on holiday even though she was upstairs in our house in Reading.

Not a bad idea. But she was having a few issues with the technicalities of wallpapering, which she realised is quite a skilled job. I think she might have had the roll the wrong way round because she had papered a row of beach huts upside down near the ceiling.

I was trying my best not to get involved with any of it. The ropeless skipping or the hopeless wallpapering. So I was chilling out in my room trying to see if I could hit a table tennis ball off the wardrobe, then the light shade and then back again. I was nailing it
– I'd done four in a row. A record.

And then, my brother started to . . .

REAM.

'It's happened. Oh my god. Oh my god,' he was shrieking. 'Big Red Cizza said it would. I'm going to be sick. I'm going to be sick. It was crunchy.' He had just woken up. And was now piling down the stairs to the toilet, where he started to make retching noises that are just best forgotten about.

My mum stopped putting adhesive on the back of a beach ball and ran down to see what was going on. My dad didn't stop skipping, though; he was up to 2,795 so he was too close to his target to stop now.

But what on earth was going on?

When I found out the truth, I slightly wished I had carried on with my furniture-based table tennis training.

My brother had accidentally eaten a **SPIDER**.

And judging by his level of panic, and the noise from the bathroom, I can only assume it had been a tarantula.

Now . . . I know what you are thinking.

What on earth has this got to do with anything? You came here to read a book about ideas, opinions and arguments. And instead, here you are reliving the day my brother chowed down on an arachnid for his breakfast.

I understand if you want to quit right now. Don't though . . . giving up isn't usually a great option. (There is an AWESOME book about that by the way. It's mega. A blockbuster. A must read. And the author is hilarious . . . well . . . he thinks he's hilarious.)

Anyway, the point is . . . I promise that there IS a point to this story. And I am getting to it.

You see, my brother's friend at school (Ciaran, aka Big Red Cizza) had told him that the average human eats EIGHT spiders in their lifetime. While asleep. The eight-legged explorers apparently walk on in to your wide-open slobbery mouth, while you are dreaming of eating that over-priced hot dog (is that just me?).

And this morning, my brother had woken up with what he thought was a spider's leg on his lip. And (Fast Thinking on overdrive) assumed that he had swallowed the seven other legs, eight eyes and a hairy body.

EWWWWWWW.

But – and here is where we get to the point – this sounded all very unlikely to me. I mean, if I use my Slow Thinking to consider this properly, it makes no sense. Spiders spend all of their time living under the floorboards actively trying to avoid humans who might stamp on them. Why would they suddenly decide to come out at night and climb up the snoring, gurgling, shaking land mass that is my sleeping brother, and end their days by falling head first in to his throat?

So, while my dad was finishing the last forty-five of his ropeless skips, I decided to take a closer look at this.

And it didn't take all that much research to find out that Big Red Cizza had been the victim of some FAKE NEWS. A guy in his football team told him about it. But this guy was the captain, and so everyone had assumed that if he had said it was true, then it must be true.

And by the time Big Red Cizza (the coolest kid in my brother's class) had repeated it with confidence to my brother, it was as good as fact. Except it wasn't. It wasn't true at all.

FAKE NEWS

Definition: information that is false even though it is being presented as news or fact.

In 2017 the Collins Dictionary made 'fake news' its word of the year.

Now, this is not a dictionary for people called Collin. This is a big player in the world of dictionaries. And so, we'll overlook the obvious issue that they don't seem to be able to count (to all the Collins . . . 'fake news' is two words, guys!).

But this does show that fake news is quite a big deal. If it is the 'word(s)' of the year, it must be quite common. It must be happening all the time. They could have chosen 'sandwich' (happening everywhere, especially in our house) or 'sofa' (a lot of those at our house too). But they didn't, they chose fake news. And it seems as though it is really common. Which is kind of worrying if you ask me. That there are people out there willing to write or say things that are just not true. But presenting them as if they are fact. With the sole purpose of making you believe in something that is just wrong.

It turns out, though, that while there is obviously a lot of FAKE news around, this isn't NEW news. Fake news has been happening for thousands of years.

Fancy a history lesson? Go on . . . bear with me . . . it will give us a rest from talking about Collin and the fact that he can't even count to two.

As far back as Roman times, fake news was used to persuade people to think in a certain way. When Octavian, the adopted son of the Roman General, Julius Caesar, wanted to be the next Roman leader, he decided to use a bit of fake news to get the people on his side and win against his opponent Mark Anthony.

He spread rumours that Mark Anthony didn't represent the values needed in a leader. That he was too busy smooching with Queen Cleopatra and getting drunk to be good at the job of ruling. Obviously, he couldn't post that online back then; it was a bit more tricky to get the message out, so he had to print it on the coins (which I suspect was a bit more expensive than a Facebook post). But the false reporting worked and Octavian – who later became known as Augustus Caesar – ended up ended up ruling for over forty years.

And it wasn't just the Romans who were at it. In 1669 a leaflet called *Strange News Out of Essex* published the details of a dragon that 'many . . . witnesses' had seen. According to the leaflet, this dragon was a winged serpent who spent its time lounging in rivers, sunning itself on hills and eating the local cows. Now . . . I don't know what was going down 350 years ago, but I have my suspicions that a sun-lounging, steak-eating monster wasn't actually roaming the streets of Essex. But the author reporting on this fantastical beast and its antics wrote about it as if it were fact. And the poor people believed it and then wasted their time on serpent-slaying expeditions.

NOT COOL!

Today, it is even easier to spread fake news. You don't have to melt the family silver (who has family silver by the way? Not the Syeds, that's for sure) and start minting coins with your messages on them. You can just post anything and everything online. And on some websites there are no checks on what is true and what is not true.

So fake news can be hard to spot. It often comes with a super-exciting headline designed deliberately to draw our attention to it. Making us think, 'Wow, this is interesting.' And before we know it, we have clicked right in to it and read it.

And it can be used to change the way we think and make decisions.

There are estimates that in the three months before the election for President of the United States in 2016, fake stories about the election between Donald Trump and Hillary Clinton were shared on Facebook 38 million times. And in 2019 the top 100 fake news stories on Facebook were viewed 150 million times.

That means all of those millions of people didn't spot that the news they were sharing was about as accurate as my mum when she's playing darts. Which is to say, totally inaccurate. She played once at our school Christmas fair. Let's just say that the deputy head walked with a limp for a while.

So don't worry if you get confused and believe something that turns out to be false. It is happening to millions of people every day.

FAKE NEWS IN THE REAL WORLD

1. Wikipedia

Have you ever copied your entire homework from a Wikipedia entry?

No? Really? You haven't ever?

Are your parents back? And reading this? I won't tell them, I promise.

OK, so you have then. I knew it.

fakenews.com

But did you know that anyone can make changes to Wikipedia entries? LITERALLY ANYONE. You could probably go on there right now and edit Justin Bieber's entry to say that you are his cousin or install yourself as the sixth Kardashian sister. It might get changed back fairly quickly, but for a while you could be on there for having invented the vacuum cleaner, built Stonehenge or ruled Europe in 1432.

fakenews.com

I know this, because someone changed my entry. They said I had a shop selling sports clothes in Hull. Best tracksuits and trainers in the North East, apparently.

If you ask me, I was a bit disappointed. It isn't the most exciting change you could think of. I mean, couldn't they have at least said that I had been a backing singer for Harry Styles? I know all of the words to 'Watermelon Sugar'.

Anyway, I don't run a sports shop. I'm not sure I have ever even been to Hull. So if you need a new pair of trainers, don't start haring up the M62 motorway to Matthew Syed Sports.

It doesn't exist. Although if it did, I'd probably be a lot better dressed than I am.

But how would you possibly know that this detail was FAKE NEWS? After all, there was a lot on there that was true. Like, I played table tennis and went to two Olympics. That I write books and am a journalist for a newspaper. That my mum is Welsh and my dad is Pakistani. And (sadly) that I've got no hair.

fakenews.com

The **TRUTH** is that it can be hard to spot the **TRUTH**.

So (and I know this could be a blow to your homework tactics in future) you might need to start looking for the evidence yourself. And not taking it for granted that everything you read online is true.

For a start, you could take a look at my trainers. They are about ten years old! And not the kind of trainers a man with his own sports shop would be wearing. And if you looked up Matthew Syed Sports online, you wouldn't find anything except some old pictures of me playing table tennis (in a bad tracksuit). If you tried calling the shop, no one would answer. In fact, you wouldn't even find a phone number.

So the evidence could help you discover that there is in fact no Matthew Syed Sports in Hull.

But isn't it amazing to think that there are people out there who have nothing better to do than change my Wikipedia page?

But someone out there did. And if they'll change my page . . . well . . . there are a lot more important people, historical events or sports shops they could find to lie about.

2. Planet Nibiru – Planet X

Have you heard of Planet Nibiru? Thought not.

But if you look online, you'll find oodles of content about Nibiru or Planet X. It is supposed to be the ninth planet in our solar system. And some reports suggest it is on a collision course with Earth.

OMG!

Now, before you start tunnelling a bunker under your house so you can hide there and wait for impact, let's take a closer look at this.

We've got two sides:

NASA – NASA scientists don't believe that a ninth planet, ten times the size of the Earth, is going to crash into our living room anytime soon. And they would consider themselves to be an authority on this sort of stuff.

Planetary Smash-Up Believers – Astronomers have been looking for a ninth planet for a long time. But the story of Nibiru began in 1976, when a book was written about a planet that we have not yet discovered and takes 3,600 years to orbit the Sun. Then in 1995 a woman called Nancy Lieder picked up the story and, applying some questionable analysis (she said she was being advised by aliens), suggested that this planet was on a collision course with Earth. She told people that the impact was going to be 27 May 2003. It was even reported in the *New York Times*. And rumour has it that she even advised people that they should sell their homes, put down their pets and get ready for the end of the world.

Guess what? **IT DIDN'T HAPPEN.**

Now, you'd think that would make Nancy and her crew have a rethink. Maybe this collision smash-up scenario thing wasn't true after all.

But it didn't. And instead a very strange thing happened. The believers felt even MORE sure that the apocalypse was coming! And instead of wondering why on earth (see what I did there!) it hadn't happened, they decided it was just going to happen later. They simply moved the date of certain death and the end of Earth as we know it and rescheduled it to 2012.

When 2012 rolled around, NASA even issued a statement saying that there was no possibility of an intergalactic smash. Because by that time NASA was receiving dozens of emails and calls every week from worried people around the world, wondering whether they should start planning their final meal.

But even the no-show in 2012 didn't deter the believers. They rescheduled again until 2017.

And again, it didn't happen. So I think after three failures they have decided to stay in their underground bunkers and leave it there. But who knows, there may still be some of them out there waiting for Nibiru to arrive and prove them right after all.

NOTE: We'll come back to this later in the book. BUT this is a very important issue for us to consider. These guys had predicted a cataclysmic end-of-the-world event . . . THAT HADN'T HAPPENED. You'd think they'd be celebrating. Getting back their old jobs that they had given up so they could build their bunkers. Buying new pets (too soon?). But they didn't. They just moved the date. And this shows you HOW HARD IT IS TO ADMIT YOU ARE WRONG. And this is true for many of us. Imagine you have told your friends and family that the world is going to end on 27 May? They've rehoused their goldfish, sold their car and said goodbye to all their friends. And then, when it doesn't happen, you've got to be the one to tell them they've cashed in their life savings for a total crackpot rumour?

No way. Easier to style it out, right? To pretend like the whole scheme is still on, you just need to wait a little while longer . . .

When you have decided to believe in something, it can be very hard to admit you might need to change your mind. This is one of the reasons it's so important to look at who or what is influencing you. If you don't question it, you could end up believing a piece of totally fake news and trying to convince everyone else it's true when it's not!

Anyway . . . back to the issue. Nibiru coming to smash into Earth was FAKE NEWS. But it was pretty widely reported online. So how could we tell it was fake?

You might be tempted to think that NASA must be right? They are the American government's space agency after all. They have got billions of dollars to go looking for this kind of stuff and they haven't found it.

BUT the 'authorities' have been wrong in the past about some fairly major space stuff. Remember (well, you won't, because it was about 490 years before you were born) that time everyone thought that the Earth was the centre of the universe?

So how do we make sure that we're not being influenced by fake news and work out what is true?

We need to look at . . . THE EVIDENCE, and then we need to decide for ourselves.

CASE 1

No one has ever seen Nibiru or Planet X. Although there is some evidence (and NASA agrees) that there might be a ninth planet in our solar system. But even if it does exist, there is no proof that it is on a collision course with Earth.

CASE 2

Reading the online stories about Nibiru, some of them seem quite believable. But ask yourself, where do these stories come from? When you dig deep enough, you discover that they originated from a woman believing she was being advised by aliens. Not exactly a reliable source.

So, some final tips on how to spot fake news . . .

TOP TIP:

1 Who is writing the story? Are they an established author or journalist? Do they have a reputation for writing crazy stories (yes, you in Essex with that leaflet about the sun-bathing, bolognese-eating beast) or real news?

2 What is the purpose of the story? Is the writer or website trying to sell you something? Sometimes you will see wild and intriguing headlines like 'Man turns into fish finger'. They are deliberately astonishing to make you click through in to the article. Only when you do, you find out you've been conned, guy just dreamt he was a fish finger and in fact they are trying to sell you a new dishwasher.

3 Can you find the story elsewhere? Does it say the same thing or is there another side to the story? Can you find the same story with the same facts in three different places?

4 Is it on a website that you have heard of? Are there spelling mistakes or grammatical errors? At a newspaper such as *The Times* (which I write for), we have a whole team of editors and fact checkers to make sure we don't print mistakes. Many of the fake news sites won't have this, so you'll spot mistakes that you wouldn't have made in Year 1!

5 Photos can be edited. The camera can definitely lie. So be careful not to assume that everything you see in a photo or a video is real.

FAKE NEWS AT SCHOOL

This happens all of the time. How often does someone tell you they haven't revised for a test and then they come out with the top mark? Maybe they want to be top of the class. Or maybe they wanted to do better than you. Either way . . . urgh . . . it was fake news.

And that party you didn't get invited to . . . did they all really have the best day ever? Was that just fake news? And was it actually like my eleventh birthday when it rained and we had to have a picnic in a multi-storey car park?

FAKE PHOTOS

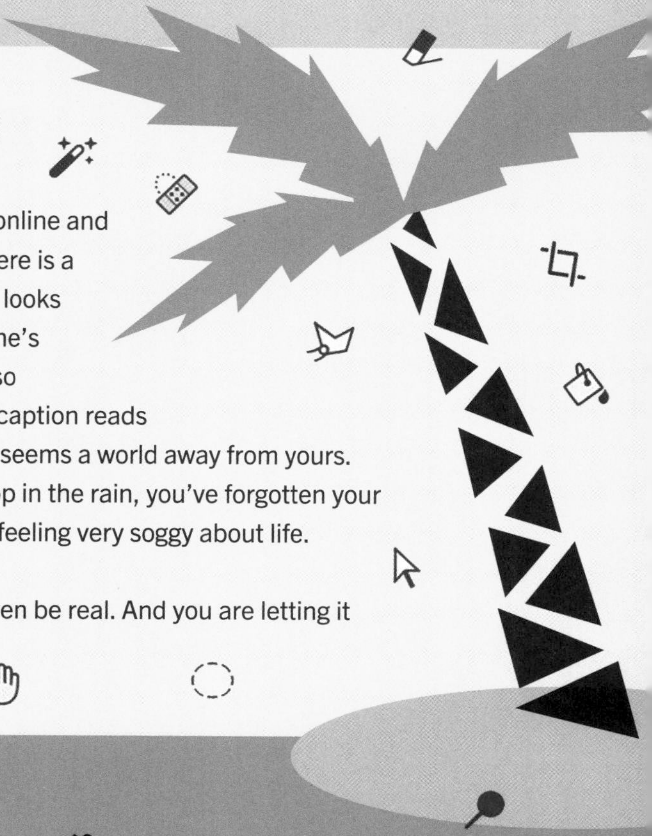

You're looking at a picture online and it is making you jealous. There is a beautiful girl. You think she looks miles better than you do. She's on an amazing beach. It is so exotic and glamorous. The caption reads 'best life ever xxx' and it all seems a world away from yours. You're at the school bus stop in the rain, you've forgotten your umbrella and are currently feeling very soggy about life.

But that photo might not even be real. And you are letting it dampen your mood.

It is so easy to 'fake' a photo. You can make the sky more blue. You can make the sand more white and the sea more sparkly. You can make your skin smoother and more tanned. Your legs longer and thinner. All with a click of a button on a mobile phone.

And what is to say that her smile is even real? If you ask me, after taking 6,534 photos and then spending another hour editing in the perfect hairstyle, I would NOT be smiling. I'd be thinking that this holiday was all a bit too much like hard work.

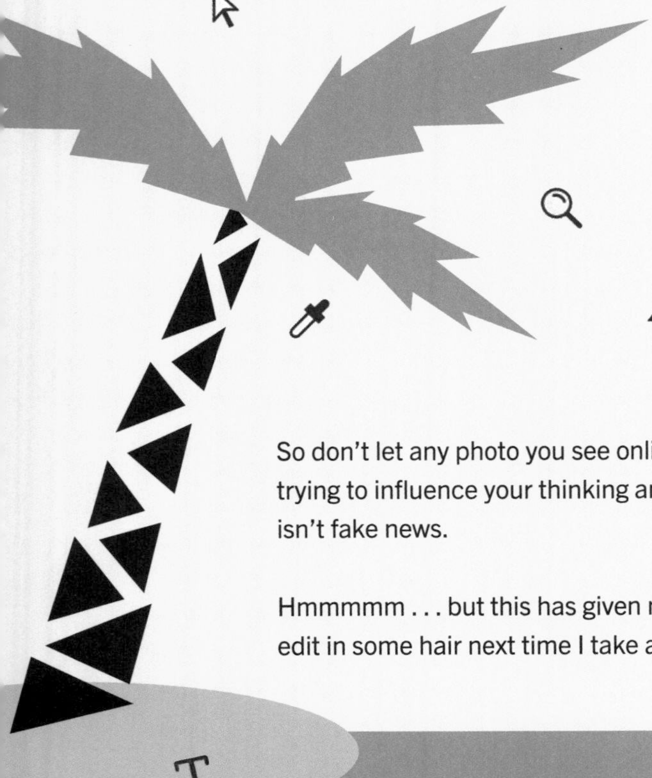

So don't let any photo you see online affect your mood. It is trying to influence your thinking and you can never be sure it isn't fake news.

Hmmmmm . . . but this has given me a brilliant idea. I might edit in some hair next time I take a selfie!

Anyway, back to my brother and the spider story. Well, that eighth leg that had remained stuck to his lip when he woke up in a panic? That turned out to be one of my dad's hairs. We knew it was his in the end because on closer inspection it smelled of his hair wax and no one else had hair thick enough to resemble a spider's leg.

Frankly, I would rather have eaten the spider.

AND THAT IS

NOT

FAKE NEWS.

PS: If you are interested in other Collins words of the year . . .

- *'Single-use' was word of the year in 2018 (nice try with the hyphen, Collin)*

- *'Climate strike' was word of the year in 2019 (you're not even trying any more, Colin)*

- *'Lockdown' was word of the year in 2020*

- *'Non-fungible token' was word of the year 2021 (seriously, Collin . . . take a maths lesson . . . this is out of control now)*

CHAPTER 4

WHY WE ARGUE

Are you still thinking about that hot dog? I am. I can't stop thinking about it.

But . . . I need to stop. Because we have got to get stuck into the rest of this book. And there are some meaty topics (seriously? . . . that isn't helping me forget it) to cover. We know about how we think and the influences out there that can anchor our opinions. But, when we have decided on our point of view, what is the best way tell other people what we think? And what do we do if they don't agree?

See . . . I told you this was important stuff. So, banish that dog of dreams from your mind . . . and let's get in to this.

CONFLICT OF INTEREST

Jack Harvey was nothing like me.

In fact, the whole Harvey family were nothing at all like the Syed family.

They were very rich. They went on holiday to places I couldn't even pronounce (I mean, they went to Taumatawhakatangihangakoauauotamateaturipukakapikimaungahoronukupokaiwhenuakitanatahu one summer. Yeah . . . me neither. Somewhere in New Zealand apparently).

They lived in a massive house. There was a rumour that it even had its own river. I was never sure whether that was fake news or not, though. I mean, how would someone own their own river? It is not like you can go out and buy one from the local Homebase. But Dominic Lyall had said he'd gone on a boat trip at half term and was sure he sailed through the Harvey's garden.

Who knows . . . but they were definitely **LOADED.**

The Syeds, on the other hand, **WERE NOT.**

While Mrs Harvey was buying her handbags in Chanel, Mrs Syed was buying hers second hand in the Oxfam charity shop. And while Jack's trainers were the latest Nike Air Jordans, mine were from Reading market and had already been worn (out) by my brother for a year before I got my feet into them.

We didn't care at all, though. I am not sure we really noticed.

That is, until me and Jack had to work together on a school project to help out a local charity. I thought that this was a great bit of homework for the Easter holidays. And it definitely beat that rainforest diorama we had to make last year. That was a nightmare. I had spent ages moulding a three-toed sloth out of modelling clay when my brother took a bite out of it thinking it was a chocolate Lindt ball. He got quite a shock and spat it out all over my tree-top canopy. The whole thing was a soggy disaster after that.

So this was much better. We could choose a local charity and write a diary of what we had done to help them out.

My mum's friend worked at the local food bank and she thought that they could use our help packing the food parcels for people who needed them. Perfect.

I put this to Jack, thinking I had solved all our problems. And he acted like a total fool.

WHY WOULD ANYONE NEED THAT? WE NEED TO DO SOMETHING FOR A PROPER CHARITY,

said Jack. He looked at me like I was the biggest idiot he had ever come across.

BUT THIS IS A PROPER CHARITY. THEY FEED THOUSANDS OF FAMILIES EVERY YEAR. CHILDREN GOING HUNGRY IS A BIG DEAL,

I said, trying to explain, but he interrupted . . .

WHAT? I'M NOT GIVING OUT FOOD TO A BUNCH OF SCROUNGERS. ARE YOU SERIOUSLY TELLING ME THAT PEOPLE CAN'T EVEN AFFORD A PACKET OF SPAGHETTI? WHY DON'T THEY JUST SELL ONE OF THEIR CARS SO THEY DON'T HAVE TO TAKE FOOD OFF OTHER PEOPLE?

WHAT? WAS HE SERIOUS?

But he really was serious.

I went mad. I totally lost it with him. I'm not proud of it but I even hit him with a twelve pack of toilet rolls that my mum had given me for a donation to the food bank. He wasn't hurt. His brand-new Adidas puffer jacket cushioned the blow. But I was so angry. I couldn't quite believe that anyone could even think that. Let alone say it out loud.

But this whole episode got me thinking. How could we have such different opinions? After all, we went to the same school, were in the same class, did the same homework. But we clearly had very different ideas about the food bank and why people might need its help.

In chapter 2 we saw that we can tend to assume that people will think like us. We can be anchored to our own set of beliefs about things and find it surprising when other people don't hold the same views.

So, let's break this down:

My anchor

My dad worked long hours as a university professor while my mum held down two jobs so we could pay for everything for our family.

We used to save money by eating dinner from tins that my mum had brought home for free after her shift stacking the shelves at Asda. They were tins that had been damaged or had lost their labels and so couldn't be sold by the supermarket. It was a total lottery on those evenings. One time we had three tins of peaches and four tins of roast chicken and one final tin that seemed to be a whole cooked breakfast in a can. I felt a bit (a lot) queasy at table tennis practice after that concoction.

We were fortunate enough not to have needed to use the food bank, but we knew a few people who had. Barry from next door used it. His wife lost her job when a local factory closed down and money was tight for a while. Their kids sometimes had to wear school uniform at the weekend because there wasn't enough money for other clothes. So I could see how helpful the food bank could be.

Jack's anchor

Jack didn't really have any neighbours. His garden (and possible river) was so large that you couldn't see anyone else around. There was a long driveway, with lights and a fountain up to his enormous house. And parked there were four cars. One of them was a Porsche. One of them was some kind of dune buggy that Jack got to drive round his massive garden.

Jack had all of the latest kit too. Trainers, clothes, sunglasses. He even had two watches. One for school and one for 'the weekend'. Who needs a weekend watch? Like telling the time might be different at the weekend or something . . .?

The point is that me and Jack were surrounded by quite different circumstances at home. And I would bet all of my table tennis balls that Jack's dad was not jumping round his living room over an imaginary skipping rope because he didn't want to spend the money on a real one. Jack's dad would have a top-of-the-range rope.

And so it wasn't that Jack was mean or nasty when he said he didn't believe that the food bank was a real charity. He just couldn't imagine how anyone would need it. He had so much money and so many expensive things that not having enough for food wasn't something he had ever even considered, let alone experienced. He just assumed that because he had four cars, everyone must have a spare car lying around that they could put on eBay if they needed to.

The Syeds, on the other hand, had only one car. A very dented Talbot Samba (with 'Syed Brothers' written on the side, but that is another story). And even if we had put it on eBay, I don't think anyone would have bought it.

So while we have a tendency to assume other people might think like us, they quite often don't. Our experiences, our culture, our background and even our goals can shape and influence what we believe and how we feel. It is like our own surroundings can make us a little bit blind to there being any other point of view out there.

Famous Blind Spots: Marie Antoinette famously said the phrase 'Let them eat cake' when she was told of the famine happening in France. The harvest had failed, rats had eaten the crops, the people had no bread and they were starving. The phrase 'Let them eat cake' showed just how out of touch the princess was with reality. If the people couldn't afford bread, they were hardly likely to be able to buy cake, which was much more expensive. It kind of ended in quite a big row too. The people revolted and chopped off her head not long afterwards. **FAKE NEWS ALERT** – although this phrase is widely attributed to Marie Antoinette, it is unlikely that *she* actually said it. The evidence shows that there are references to it in French history almost a hundred years before Marie Antoinette. So it was more likely to have been said by a different (but still deluded) princess.

GRAVE DANES

A similar thing happened when Anders Mortenson came to stay with us from Denmark. He was a Danish table tennis player who had heard that the Syed brothers might be good to train against. We would have been, but we had a row on the first night and he went to stay with Jimmy Stokes instead.

'Come on, man,' he was saying as we all finished up with our spin serve session. 'I've read about it. I can't wait to get down there.'

'Where?' I hadn't been listening. I assumed he meant the local park or McDonald's. Maybe he wanted in on the Big Mac detour me and Jimmy Stokes sometimes did on the way home.

'Reading Cemetery, obviously,' he said, as if me and my brother were complete fools. He was so excited. 'I have looked it up. It is huge. I can't wait.'

This was the weirdest thing I had ever heard. And in the Syed family that has got a lot of competition.

I checked. It was a windy Wednesday in April. It wasn't Halloween. Why on earth would he want to get the bus to the graveyard three miles away?

'That sounds like a terrible idea,' my brother said.

'Yeah, why would anyone want to do that? Why don't we go to the cinema?' I replied

'But I have come here to party,' he insisted, getting angry. 'I don't need you losers cramping my style. And I don't want to watch any stupid cartoon.'

CHARMING!

But off he went. In a huff because we wouldn't join him on the orange 14 bus to the cemetery.

We didn't see him again until the European Championships in August, when he came racing over before his match.

'I am SO sorry, Syeds,' he said (like me and my brother were one person). 'The cemetery was rubbish. Just graves everywhere. And loads of crows.'

'Yeah . . .' I said, thinking that this was the most obvious statement in history (except the bit about the crows, which was a surprise). 'What exactly did you expect?'

It turns out that he was expecting a party.
People hanging out. Having fun.

Because that is what happens in Denmark. Apparently the local graveyard is the place to be and be seen. The place to go and meet your friends (not that Anders had any in Reading, he only knew us and Jimmy, and he ditched us pretty quickly). So while we were thinking a night out at the cemetery sounded like the spookiest idea of all time, Anders thought it would be where he had all his fun.

Our experiences and culture meant that we had totally different views about where to hang out and have a good time.

Don't Pick a Fight

Different cultures have traditions that might seem unusual to us. But . . . unlike me and Anders Mortenson, sometimes it's better to avoid arguing about what is better or who is right and respect that people have different ways of doing things.

Did You Know?

In Ethiopia it is common to put food in the mouths of the other people you are eating dinner with. But what would you think if you were sitting down to eat, then the guy sitting next to you tried to stuff a piece of chicken in your mouth?

In Venezuela it is considered greedy to arrive on time to a party. Like you might want to get your hands on the best party food before anyone else arrives. So, in order to respectful, everyone turns up at least 15 minutes late and sometimes much later than that. So if punctuality is not your strong point move to Caracas, they'll think you are super polite.

CONFLICTS OF CHOICE

Having choices is awesome. And for many of us, over the past few decades, we have more and more choices than ever. Choices about where we might live, the type of job we might do or the kind of person we might marry. Awesome! Being able to choose a career, or no longer having to do certain chores around the house just because you're a boy or a girl is great. It means we can live our best lives. But . . . it does make it more likely that we might choose to do or think something that others don't like or agree with. Football and tennis were the two sports on offer at my school. But then Mr Charters arrived and started a table tennis club. More choice! Brilliant. But my football coach didn't agree, he was furious. He wanted me on the football team but I didn't have time to do both, so I chose table tennis.

Another example of where more choice can provoke more arguments is politics. In the UK we get to vote on who runs the country. We get to choose our government because we live in a democracy. But this isn't the case everywhere in world. In North Korea nobody gets a vote. There is no choice at all. The ruler (currently Kim Jong-un) gets to decide on everything that happens in the country and no one can challenge him. He's decided that you'll go to jail if you watch a Western movie. iPhones and iPads are banned. And if you are a man who likes a longer hairstyle, then watch out because Kim Jong-Un only likes short hair like his. No arguments. You're not allowed anything longer than 5 cm. So if you want to go full Harry Styles, this might not be place for you.

So we are very lucky. We have a system we've developed over thousands of years where you can choose the government and your haircut. And while this is brilliant, it can of course lead to disagreements. And I don't mean about whether to have a bob or braids. I mean about which leader is best, about whether they'll improve the NHS or spend enough money on climate change. And people can fall out big time over these issues.

All this tells us that arguments are to be expected. They are totally normal and happen every day. And that as we have more information and opportunities to choose the things we do and believe in, it is inevitable that we will bump into people who don't agree with us.

THE MOST IMPORTANT THING IS THAT WE DON'T LET THE ROWS GET OUT OF CONTROL.

Unlike the ones I have with my brother. Which always start nicely and get wild very quickly.

Like this one . . .

What's the most important subject at school?
ME
P.E. Obviously.
HIM

I'm more of a maths kind of guy myself. Think it will be useful when I start a business.

ME

Why? What kind of business do you want to start?

HIM
(laughing)

Errrr . . . I don't know. Maybe a sportswear business.

ME

What would you know about good sportswear? You've been wearing that yellow shell suit for four days straight.

HIM

It's called style.

ME

What about your hairy toes? Are they part of your style too?

HIM

And we are now wrestling on the floor. My mum is having to separate us. And I am wondering whether I need to shave my toes.

ARGUMENTS VS ARGUMENTS

Did you know, the word 'argument' has two meanings in the dictionary:

1. the act or process of arguing, reasoning or discussing
2. an angry quarrel or disagreement

And the issue is that any argument can move from a reasonable discussion (definition 1) to an angry personal fight where people say and do things that are really insulting and nasty (definition 2) very quickly.

arguments.com

The internet doesn't help with this either. While it is great that everyone has much more access to news and information than ever before in history, it is also very easy to find things you don't agree with online. And get into mega rows with people you don't even know. They can start off quite sensibly, but can easily turn nasty. It can be easy to hurl insults at people online when you disagree and no one has to deal with the consequences of their nasty words. People can just walk away from the screen and never have to see just how upset they have made someone else with their unkind words.

HOW TO ROW
(OR WHAT I LIKE TO CALL . . . THE HAIRY TOE TEST)

We're going to get into arguments. That is one thing we know for sure now. But when we do, we want to make sure that we are debating and questioning. Probing someone else's view to see whether they might actually be right. And we might learn something. Or we might teach them something if our point of view is different.

But we must try hard not to let it get nasty.

My brother could never quite resist an insult. Maybe it was to make me feel a bit unsure of myself so I might come round to his way of thinking. Maybe he couldn't think of any more good points to make about the issue we were arguing about. I don't know. But it has always made me think hard before I say anything personal.

So . . . if you are about to say something about someone's hairy toes . . . think twice and maybe take a look at these top tips for having a reasonable disagreement:

Respect their point of view

Always remember that it is OK for people to have a different view to you. And after reading this book, you'll have a much better understanding of why that might be the case.

Try (nicely) to debate. See if you can get them to understand your point of view, and maybe even change their view as a result. If you can't, then respect the fact that not everyone out there is going to agree with you all of the time.

Stay on topic

Don't try and 'win' the argument by getting angry or scornful of your friends' views. And never resort to personal insults. Keep reminding yourself of the point you are arguing about and keep the conversation to that.

Don't dwell on it afterwards

If you have managed to keep calm and get your point across, don't overthink things afterwards. After all, it is unlikely you want to fall out permanently.

And . . . if someone has said something nasty about the size of your nose or the hairiness of your toes . . . then try to ignore it and remember that arguments can make nice people say horrible stuff that they don't mean.

Don't shy away, though . . .

Don't try and keep the peace by not saying your piece. If you have a view, it is important that you feel heard. So have the confidence to speak up and make your point.

CHAPTER 5

SHALL WE AGREE TO DISAGREE?

So, we've been through a lot together in this book already. You've been forced to consider whether I have more hair on my toes than on my head (I don't). You've pictured my dad skipping in our living room without a skipping rope. And you know to head straight to the cemetery next time you visit Denmark.

I mean . . . what more could you ask for from a book?

But seriously, I think we have learned quite a bit too. Come on . . . we have. We now know to:

SLOW DOWN – We understand much more about the way we think, and the fact that our Fast Thinking can sometimes lead us to jump to conclusions or form opinions that might not be quite right. We need to engage our Slow Thinking.

DITCH THE ANCHOR – We can see that our views can be influenced by anchors, our experiences and our background. We should recognise what's influencing us and challenge it.

REVIEW THE EVIDENCE – We know that we have to be careful and look at the evidence before we decide what we think, sifting out any fake news as we go along. We should work out what's true and what's fake news so our actions are not influenced by something untrue.

EXPECT TO ARGUE – We know that we are highly likely to get into arguments from time to time. But we know that we should do it in a controlled way and not get personal.

NOW, LET'S MOVE THIS THING ON . . .

What if it turned out that arguing was actually quite a good thing? What if it could even make you smarter?

Really?

So rolling around the floor with my brother, shouting about toes that might require a hairdresser is to be encouraged? It might make me do better in my maths test next week?

NO . . . not THAT KIND of arguing. I'm talking about a clash of ideas. A debate to see who has the most insight and information. A discussion, back and forth. With all sides listening to see whether they can contribute or, better still, learn something new.

The skill is getting good at *this* kind of arguing . . . and I will let you in to a secret: this skill is seriously useful if you want to. . .

- be prime minister (you probably don't, but they tend to be good at this)
- negotiate a pay rise when you get a job
- get your point across in the playground
- convince your mum and dad to buy you a new mobile phone
- encourage your brother to share the secret sweet stash under his bed

DEBATABLE DAD

I owe a lot to my dad. He died in 2021, so I can't tell him that any more, but I do.

Luckily I don't think I have inherited his love of a reclining leather sofa. And I am aware that skipping without a rope is something that everyone else in the world calls . . . jumping!

But he believed in some things that are so important and have helped me in ways he will never know. He believed that if you want something you have to work hard enough to make it happen.

He also believed that his voice should be heard. He had come to England from Pakistan at a time when sadly there were a lot of people who didn't place as much value as they should on the opinions of someone with his skin colour. He didn't always get promoted at work when he was good enough. And people didn't always listen to his views and take him as seriously as they should have.

But that didn't put him off making his point. He was always calm. But he would make sure he was heard. And even if people didn't always agree with him, he would make sure they had listened to what he had to say.

He helped me **LEARN HOW TO ARGUE.**

Because he loved a debate. Around the kitchen table. On the sofa (in full recline mode). In the car (which was dangerous – he was a man who needed to fully focus on his driving otherwise a pile-up was likely). On the phone. In a shop, which could be awkward . . . he'd always ask the check-out assistant what they thought.

'Do you think the government should be closing the coal mines? What about all of the miners who will lose their jobs? How will they retrain to do other jobs?' he'd ask the guy behind the till.

These were **BIG** questions. And we were in a pet shop in Reading.

'Mate . . . I just work here. So do you want the dog flea powder or not?'

And this is how it would often go. But my dad didn't care. He was genuinely interested in what other people thought. He felt he might learn something new.

And quite often he did. He once spent two hours debating the United States presidential election with a guy from the car insurance company. (This time) He had crashed into a swan. I didn't think it would be an easy conversation trying to explain that one. But it turned out the guy from the insurance company was also from Pakistan and had an interest in the voting system in America. My dad came off the phone with a budget to fully fix the car and a new perspective on Barack Obama.

TAKING THEIR SIDE!

The other thing my dad did was make me and my brother switch sides during an argument.

So, we'd be discussing the benefits of the Reading FC back four defenders versus the Manchester United back four (my brother loved United) and dad would make us switch. I'd have to see whether I could find the positives in the United line-up and the weaknesses with Reading's players.

I didn't enjoy that much, but it definitely made me realise that there were problems with Reading's back four that I hadn't considered before. And that maybe (and that's a BIG maybe) there were some good players at United.

Another time we were talking about whether you would rather have eternal life or live until you are 100 but have a really wonderful time.

My brother was adamant he wanted to live for ever. Why not? Just think of all of the ice cream you could eat. And Manchester United were bound to win at least one trophy if you have eternity to wait.

He was pretty convinced. And I thought he was going to start getting annoyed and start saying insulting things about my tracksuit when my dad made us switch sides. All of a sudden he was forced to think through a different point of view. Maybe life would get boring if you ate ice cream and watched football every day for ever. And maybe it wouldn't be much fun if you got so old you couldn't walk any more.

My brother didn't change his mind totally. He still thought that being around for the future to watch *Mission Impossible 6,898,000* or have a holiday on Neptune would be a good thing. But he did admit that he wouldn't look forward to it quite as much if he got so old that he couldn't walk to his spaceship.

Looking at an argument from the opposite point of view can be massively helpful. It makes you think about the holes and weaknesses in your own views. If you know in advance what the other side might throw at you, then you can be prepped and ready to make your argument stronger. Or it might even mean you change your mind completely.

And this helped us out A LOT.

We needed new table tennis tables at school. And I was really keen to have a permanent place to practise at lunchtime. We kept having to wheel out old, broken tables into the dining hall while the kitchen staff were still wiping baked beans off the floor. And by the time we got started, we usually only had ten minutes before the bell went.

I knew that Mr Reynolds, the headmaster, was going to say no. He preferred drama and theatre to sports, and I knew that he would prefer to spend any spare school money on lighting for the next musical production. One year we didn't have any table tennis balls at school but there was still loads of money available for an extravagantly designed set for the annual Christmas musical.

So before I asked him, I thought about his point of view. And considered all of the reasons why he was going to say no. Like the fact that the school already had football pitches, tennis courts and cricket nets, and needed to provide alternatives for students who preferred arts to sports. Like the fact that it was really just me and my brother who wanted to practise table tennis every lunchtime.

I was so nervous when I went to talk to Mr Reynolds. As I walked into his office, he was singing 'Memory', a song from the musical *Cats*. He was holding a calculator as a microphone and putting a lot of feeling into it. So it was a struggle to break his rhythm and start talking about table tennis.

And, as expected, he said no. He said that the school was struggling for money and anything left over had to go towards building a replica of St Paul's Cathedral for the set of the upcoming *Mary Poppins* musical.

But I was well prepped. I had anticipated this and was ready.

So I put it to him. If we got two new tables and a special bouncy floor (there is a lot of jumping around in table tennis), then:

1. He could use the bouncy floor for the expressive dance club that ran on Wednesdays after school.
2. Me and my brother would start a table tennis club. It is a brilliant sport for getting lots of people involved.
3. We would also hold an exhibition for parents to come and watch.
4. We would charge a small entrance fee and the proceeds could all go to towards the construction of a papier-mâché St Paul's Cathedral.

I could see the confusion in his eyes. He was so certain this was a non-starter, but my arguments had made him stop singing and think twice.

And then he agreed!

Everyone was happy. We got to practise every lunchtime, and the table tennis club was a major success. The exhibition raised enough for St Paul's and there was even some extra left over for pigeons. They were a bad idea, though. They caused chaos midway through the 'Feed the Birds' number when they got too excited and pooped all over the stage.

So, what is the moral of this story? Yes . . . you definitely don't want to release live pigeons during the school play if you have any spare cash. BUT . . . what I really mean is DON'T BE NERVOUS. If there is something you feel passionately about, get out there and

ARGUE FOR IT.

FANTASTIC FIGHTING

Fight or Flight?

Did you know that we have aeroplanes because of some awesome arguments?

Orville and Wilbur Wright were two brothers from Dayton, Ohio, in the United States. And on 17 December 1903 they conquered a problem that humankind had been grappling with for thousands of years. How to fly.

The Wright brothers solved the problem of how to keep a motorised aeroplane in flight. But interestingly, they weren't engineers. They didn't have maths degrees. They weren't even experts in physics – all the things you would expect from someone if they were going to build an aeroplane.

But they did have something quite unique. Their father, Milton Wright, was very interested in debate and arguing. A lot like my dad, it seems.

Milton was a bishop in the local Christian church. But he filled his house with books about different religions. He wanted to understand the points of view of people who believed different things to him.

And he encouraged his children to discuss and debate too. And . . . guess what . . . he would often make them argue the other side's point of view to see if there was anything they could learn. A bit like my dad (which is making me wonder when me and my brother are going to change the world with a mega-important invention).

Milton Wright brought home a toy helicopter for his boys one day. They were fascinated by the propeller and how it worked. And when they broke it, they worked together to fix it. This sparked a lifelong interest in human flight.

But the Wright brothers argued. **All. The. Time.** Their disagreements about the workings of an aeroplane could go on for weeks at a time. And, according to their sister Katharine, they could be very loud and quite heated. One argument was so intense and they were both so convincing that by the end of it Orville thought Wilbur was right and Wilbur thought Orville was right.

But although they argued, they didn't see it as a dispute or as a reason to fall out. They saw it as a way of testing their ideas, of pushing their designs to the next level by having them picked apart.

'Discussion brings out new ways of looking at things,' said Wilbur.

These arguments eventually led them to the conclusion that an aeroplane would require two propellers, and to a design that would take flight in Kitty Hawk in the United States in late 1903.

Their father flew just once in one of their aeroplanes before his death. As the craft soared in the sky, 100 metres above the ground, the proud Milton Wright shouted to his son . . .

'Higher, Orville, Higher.'

Business Battles

Have you ever heard of Warren Buffett? He is a pretty rich guy. When I last checked, he had £77,000,000,000 in the bank. And I am guessing he might have even more by now.

He made his first investments when he was just eleven years old and has been successfully investing in and buying companies for more than seventy years.

He's got some unusual ideas, though. And I suspect they might be the secret to some of his success.

Usually when someone like Warren (can we call him by his first name?) considers buying a company, they would hire someone to advise them if it is a good idea. After all, you don't want to do what I did. Go putting all of your money into the Andrew Syed Doughnut Company, only to discover that the company's manager (called Andrew Syed AKA my brother) has eaten ALL of the doughnuts and doesn't have any left to sell at the school fair. (He said we'd make a fortune. He wasn't even sorry. Apparently, they tasted so good he couldn't resist. All fifteen of them. And yes, in case you are wondering, I am still mad. And he still owes me £15.67.)

Anyway, back to Warren. He doesn't just hire one person, he hires two separate people to advise him. One to tell him all of the good things about the company, like why he should buy it and how much money he will make. And then he hires someone else to argue the opposite. To tell him all of the reasons why it is a terrible idea. Why he'll make less money than the Andrew Syed Doughnut Company (which went bankrupt after less than a day).

And guess what (here is the genius bit). Each advisor only gets paid if they win the argument. So they are super keen to explain ALL of the reasons why they might be right.

But this way, Wozza (maybe we are not familiar enough for nicknames?) can be sure that he has all of the arguments and points of view in front of him when he makes a decision. And the debate will likely throw up ideas and issues that no one has thought of yet too.

These arguments are what makes Warren's business brain sharper. And his bank balance bigger.

SPEAK UP

So, arguments can make you smarter and potentially richer, and can possibly mean you might invent a world-changing method of transport like the Wright brothers.

But don't worry . . . even if you don't invent flying cars before someone at Google manages it . . . arguments can be really helpful if done in the right way.

So don't think of it as an insult, or a problem, if someone presents an alternative view. Take it as an opportunity to see if there is an idea you haven't considered. Remember that we don't just get our ideas from our own brains. We get them from arguing with each other too.

Did You Know?
The reason why humans rule the world? It is not because we are the strongest animal round here. Gorillas or bears or lions could have pulverised us years ago. And it is not because we have the biggest brains either. Elephants' brains are three times the size of ours, but you don't see them performing a heart transplant. So what is going on? How come the weedy, small-brained humans have managed to harness fire, invent mobile phones and create the Big Mac.

Well, the reason we have managed world domination is because we have a unique ability to SHARE and BUILD on what we know. To use the knowledge that has been passed down to us from our parents and grandparents to invent new and better ways of doing things with every generation.

Humans have collected a massive amount of knowledge over the course of our history. So vast that it can't be contained in any single person's brain. Your brain knows some stuff, for example, but you don't know everything (I hate to break it to you). My brain might know some other stuff, and some of that might be the same as your stuff, but a lot of it will be different. And Jeff Bezos will know totally different (and probably better) stuff to either of us.

If the three of us (you, me and Jeff Bezos, imagine that meet-up) share and build on what we know, then together we will be smarter than we would have been if we'd stayed on our own. And if everyone in the world (all seven billion of us) are all sharing and improving what we know, then . . . we will know absolutely LOADS.

Think of it like this . . . your grandma used to have a telephone. I bet it looked a bit like this:

It was probably fixed to her wall with a big wire too. And (unless your grandma was Alexander Graham Bell . . . #unlikely) she probably didn't know exactly how the phone worked. Or how on earth to make a phone. Those bits of information were in someone else's brain. But your grandma was able to use it and got the benefit of the fact that humans had invented it and then shared it.

Great . . . and while she was teaching you that phone calls are a nice way to stay in touch with your family, some other humans (maybe Mrs Android or Mr Apple) were having the new idea that maybe we could ditch the big old wire and take these things off the wall and put them in our pockets. They built on something we already had and made it better. And then that new invention of 'mobile' phones was also shared with everyone.

And by the way . . . the people that invented the mobile phone . . . well, they will have benefitted from other inventions that they didn't think of. Like cars or forks or nose-hair trimmers. It is win-win being human!

We really are able to work together and share our ideas. And, crucially, we do that best when we DEBATE, DISCUSS AND ARGUE to reveal exactly what each of us knows so that we can share our thoughts and use all of that knowledge to invent stuff, which we can use to make our lives better.

Elephants, gorillas, bears can't do this. They don't learn from each other like we do and pass that on to their children. And that is one reason why they don't have mobile phones, and why they are not currently manning the International Space Station.

SPEAK **UP** . . . CONTINUED

Now, all of this has got me (slow) thinking . . . should we actually be STARTING an argument? If having a bit of a row is so brilliant, then are there actually times when that might be a good thing to do?

If you ask my mum that question, I suspect she would say (scream, probably), 'Absolutely not!' because she will have visions of the time my brother found a mushroom growing under our bunk beds and started a massive fight about why it was there. It ended up in a wrestle on the floor (again), and this time I accidentally put my foot through the TV screen. It was bad . . . my mum missed fourteen episodes of *Countdown* before it got fixed. She's never been the same at the numbers round since.

But, back to the point, scientists who have studied groups of people to see how they make decisions have found that the groups who don't discuss or debate issues are not as good at problem-solving as those that do. Basically, groups that argue tend to make better decisions.

Why? Because when they argue, these groups are thinking through the pros and the cons of their ideas. They don't just follow the loudest person in the group and do whatever they think is right. They share their knowledge to come up with the best solution.

So **YES . . . SPEAK UP . . .** start the debate . . . and don't be afraid to get your thoughts out there. After all, you are almost certain to know things that other people in the group don't. They might even learn something from you. But stick to the ideas and don't get personal.

And if you are wondering about that mushroom – the one growing under my bed – it appeared mysteriously after my brother spilt a Bombay Bad Boy Pot Noodle. We were having a midnight feast to celebrate his table tennis win over Alan Cook when he demonstrated his forehand chop and some of the Bad Boy slurped off the top bunk on to the carpet . . . so I have my suspicions about who was to blame for that **FUNGUS.**

CHAPTER 6

WHEN ROWS GO WRONG

Did you know that 3.18 p.m. is the most likely time for a family fallout on Christmas Day?

Well, the Syeds didn't even make it to 9.18 a.m.

Apparently, most family rows happen after the turkey has been served. And the most common cause is either who has to do the washing up or who has cheated at Monopoly. Did you really roll three double sixes and land on Mayfair? You know the sort of thing . . .

Not in the Syed house, though.

We were done and dusted (and busted) before anyone had changed out of the matching penguin PJs my mum had got us all wearing. She had made them herself and no one had a pair that fitted. The arms were so long on mine they had got tangled in the night and I woke up in a panic because I couldn't find my hands.

Anyway, the row wasn't about the pyjamas.

It was about Beryl's new boyfriend.

And it was **MASSIVE.** The row. Not the boyfriend.

Beryl is my aunt. My mum's sister. I had always admired her. She was a free spirit and she seemed to have so many exciting adventures. While we were debating the colour of reclining leather sofas, Auntie Beryl was abseiling in the Andes in Argentina.

My dad thought that Auntie Beryl should come back home and get a job. But Beryl didn't listen to anyone. She was happy to live her life exactly as she wanted to.

Auntie Beryl was awesome.

And she had recently come to stay for Christmas. But unexpectedly, she had not arrived alone on Christmas Eve. Instead she had brought Carlos. Her new boyfriend from California.

This threw up a fair few problems. Not least because my mum had not made a pair of penguin pyjamas for Carlos. And we were already a bit stretched on the Christmas pudding front, so we were going to have to hope that a heap of sticky raisins was not Californian Carlos's dessert of choice.

But we were soon to discover that the pudding and the pyjamas were the least of our problems.

Carlos, it turned out, had some strong views. And was not afraid to share them.

The discussion started on Christmas Eve. We had all changed into the pyjamas, ready to sit down and watch a movie. Carlos had to make do with an apron my mum had found in the drawer. It had a polar bear on it, rather than a penguin, but my mum had said it was all she could manage at short notice.

ALL THIS BUSINESS ABOUT THESE POLAR BEARS IS TOTAL NONSENSE, RIGHT?'

I wasn't sure what he was talking about to start with. But he carried on . . .

YOU KNOW, THAT ALL THEIR ICE IS MELTING AND THEY AREN'T GOING TO HAVE A HOME THIS TIME NEXT YEAR,

he said.

I MEAN, CRY ME A RIVER. IT IS ALL TOTAL RUBBISH.

Hmmmmmm . . . 'cry me a river'? Isn't that their exact problem right there? As the earth is heating up, their nice home on the ice shelf is rapidly turning into something about as solid as the Thames estuary.

I couldn't quite work it out. Did this guy not think climate change was real?

Carlos seemed quite sure of himself. He'd even taken my dad's favourite seat on the sofa and was playing with the remote-control recliner settings. My dad was on a deck chair in the corner of the room looking increasingly furious with him.

My brother was the first to ask him about why he believed this.

BUT CARLOS, WHY DO YOU THINK IT IS TOTAL RUBBISH? THE ICE IS MELTING. IF WE CARRY ON AT THIS RATE, THEN THERE WILL BE NO ICE LEFT IN THE ARCTIC BY 2040.

This was about the most sensible thing my brother had said since he told Anders Mortenson that a night out in Reading Cemetery was a bad idea. But Carlos just looked at him and laughed. The mood in the room was turning a bit cold (pun . . . not intended). My mum tried to lift the atmosphere with a plate of mince pies for everyone. But Carlos thought they were all for him and just took the entire plate, put it on his lap and filled his mouth with a whole mince pie. He swallowed it down in one gulp and piled in a second. And then a third.

LOVE RAISINS,

was, I think, what he kept saying. His mouth was too stuffed to hear him properly. This didn't bode well for the Christmas Pudding shortage we had coming down the track tomorrow.

WHO. WAS. THIS. GUY?

YOU DO REALISE ALL THIS CLIMATE NONSENSE IS JUST PART OF THE EARTH'S NATURAL CYCLE, DON'T YOU? WE'VE BEEN COOLING DOWN AND HEATING RIGHT UP FOR MILLIONS OF YEARS NOW. WHEN THE DINOSAURS WERE AROUND, THERE WERE PALM TREES GROWING NEAR THE SOUTH POLE IT WAS SO HOT. IT'S SO MUCH COOLER NOW I DON'T KNOW WHAT WE'RE WORRIED ABOUT. WE'RE ACTUALLY IN BETWEEN ICE AGES AT THE MOMENT.

Now, this was something I didn't know. Was it fake news or was Carlos right about this? I wanted to understand his point of view, so I had a look at the evidence. Turns out Carlos was right – we are currently in what is called an interglacial period between ice ages.

I had learned something. But when my dad weighed in, I realised Carlos was missing some important pieces of the puzzle. While my dad wasn't quite Greta Thunberg, he did have a compost heap and even recycled his hair when he went to the barbers (yes, that is an actual thing you can do).

Now, my dad was very keen to meet new people. He loved hearing their stories and discussing their views. But there was just something about Carlos. He was totally unwilling to listen to anything anyone said.

BUT CARLOS

my dad said,

WHILE YOU'RE RIGHT THAT WE MIGHT BE HEADING TOWARDS AN ICE AGE IN THE FUTURE, GLOBAL WARMING HAS PROBABLY PUT THAT OFF FOR ANOTHER FIFTY THOUSAND YEARS. AND IN THE MEANTIME THE SEAS ARE RISING. FAST.

My dad was trying to point out calmly that we are basically heading for disaster.

But Carlos was having **NONE OF IT.**

Polishing off his fourth mince pie while spilling a tonne of crumbs, he said,

WE NEED TO CHILL, MAN. SOMETIMES THE EARTH IS JUST HOTTER THAN AT OTHER TIMES.

He couldn't seem to see the irony of what he was saying.

My dad tried again to be reasonable,

YOU MIGHT BE RIGHT, CARLOS, BUT IF WE KEEP ADDING TO CARBON EMISSIONS AND TEMPERATURES KEEP RISING, THEN WHOLE CITIES ARE GOING TO SINK. THE CITY OF JAKARTA IN INDONESIA COULD BE THE FIRST TO GO. AND TEN MILLION PEOPLE LIVE THERE.

At this point Carlos started to get a bit testy. And a bit angry. And then he just got plain weird.

YOU GUYS HAVE BOUGHT THE TOTAL DOOMSTER RUBBISH. SAD . . . BECAUSE BERYL TOLD ME YOU WERE SOUND.

He shouted,

WHY CAN'T YOU SEE THAT THIS WHOLE THING IS MADE UP? WHY DO YOU THINK WE STILL GET SNOW IN WINTER? GUYS, TAKE OFF YOUR GLASSES!

No one was wearing any glasses.

I thought my dad's jaw was going to hit the bottom of his deck chair.

But Carlos still wasn't finished . . .

YEAH, CAN'T YOU SEE WHAT IS REALLY GOING ON? THESE GUYS SAYING THAT EVERYTHING IS GETTING HOTTER . . . THEY ARE OUT TO GET US. THEY WANT US TO SPEND ALL OF OUR MONEY ON FANCY GADGETS TO REDUCE EMISSIONS AND EXTRA ON ELECTRICITY THAT IS MADE FROM A GRAPE OR SOMETHING WHILE THEY CARRY ON BURNING ALL THEIR COAL AND MAKING NICE CHEAP CARS FOR THEMSELVES.

CAN I SHOW YOU SOME OF THE NEWS ON THIS, CARLOS? my mum said.

THERE ARE LOTS OF PEOPLE OUT THERE WITH A DIFFERENT POINT OF VIEW ON THIS.

THE NEWS IS FULL OF IDIOTS WHO BELIEVE THE SAME RUBBISH AS YOU,

he spat back a half-chewed raisin in the direction of my dad.

WHY WOULD I READ THAT? I STICK WITH MY CREW. WE KNOW THE TRUTH.

And with that, he stormed upstairs and didn't come down again. I heard him later, on the phone. 'Chad, man, you are not going to believe what these dudes think. Total losers, man.' he was saying, and laughing.

When we got up the next morning, he and Beryl were getting ready to leave. But not before he had downed a very hasty bowl of Fruit 'n Fibre. That guy really did love a raisin.

As he left, my dad, who I think was in shock, but quite relieved that he wasn't going to have any challenge for his sofa from now on, said,

I HOPE WE MIGHT SEE YOU AGAIN. MAYBE WE CAN TALK MORE?

NO CHANCE,

said Carlos, with his back to my dad.

I HAVE ALL THE EVIDENCE I NEED. CONSIDER YOURSELF CANCELLED.

And off they went. At 9.17 a.m. In their massive diesel car. And he was still wearing the polar bear apron.

9:17 AM

That guy was a **NIGHTMARE!**

My dad spent the rest of Christmas Day in a state confusion.

WHAT DOES HE MEAN, I AM CANCELLED? he kept asking.

IS HE SAYING THAT HE NEVER WANTS TO TALK TO ME EVER AGAIN?

Yep. That is exactly what he is saying, Dad.

BUT WHY?

For my dad, who loved to debate ideas and understand other people's views, even if he didn't agree with them, he couldn't understand Carlos's behaviour.

BUT HE DIDN'T EVEN WANT TO LISTEN TO WHAT I HAD TO SAY?

Nope. He didn't, Dad.

SO HE'S STORMED OFF TO SPEND CHRISTMAS WITH PEOPLE WHO THINK JUST LIKE HE DOES?

Yep. That's exactly what he's done, Dad.

AND HE THINKS I AM AN IDIOT, AND JUST BECAUSE I DIDN'T AGREE WITH HIM ON CLIMATE CHANGE,

HE THINKS EVERYTHING I HAVE EVER DONE IN MY LIFE IS USELESS?

Yep, Dad. That is correct.

BUT THAT ISN'T FAIR.

No, Dad. It isn't.

Oh man . . .
this could go on for ever.

DAD, HE IS IN AN ECHO CHAMBER,

I said in the end.

HE DOESN'T WANT TO LISTEN.

But this didn't help either.

WHAT ON EARTH IS AN ECHO CHAMBER? IS HE A BAT?

my dad replied, even more confused.

CHAMBER DANGER

Do you know what an **ECHO CHAMBER** is?

No? Well, you and my dad are in the same place on this then. I am hoping you are not also jumping around your room without a skipping rope, though . . .

So, it isn't anything to do with bats. And it isn't a creaky bathroom where you can sing in the shower and hear your own voice bouncing off the walls.

An echo chamber is more of a situation that people get themselves in to, rather than a place you might visit. These situations can happen within groups of friends, at home and especially online.

And we can end up in the chamber without even realising it sometimes.

An echo chamber happens when you surround yourself with people who think just like you do. Your own way of thinking is being echoed back to you by others who think the same. You seek out opinions and views that mirror your own.

This chamber is not sounding like a bad place to be, right? No arguing, no fighting, everyone agreeing and telling you that you are right.

It sounds quite comforting. A place where you might feel good about yourself because you are always in the right.

BUT . . . can you see the **DANGER?**

Yes. You will never hear the other side of the debate. You'll never be able to learn from anyone who might have a different point of view because, well, you won't even talk to them. All of the good things about arguing that we heard about in chapter 5 can't happen in an echo chamber.

And you might end up like Carlos.

And I don't mean eating too many mince pies in a polar bear apron. I mean only making friends with people who don't believe in climate change, laughing at anyone else who doesn't agree with you. Deciding that everyone else is an idiot and refusing to listen to anyone else's point of view.

SOCIAL (MEDIA) SCIENCE

Social media platforms can sadly make it easier to fall into echo chambers.

Don't get me wrong. These platforms can be awesome. You can connect with people from all over the world. People just like you. People different to you. There is so much news and there are so many views out there that we can learn from. And we have access to more information than ever before. That can be amazing.

But we need to be careful.

And we need not to be Carlos.

Because, you see, these platforms don't really care all that much WHAT people read on their sites. They could be looking at cute pictures of cats, last week's football goals or dodgy information about climate change. The platforms aren't bothered. They just like people to be there, and as often as possible. Looking at adverts. The more people see those, the more money the platforms and websites make.

These online social media companies have figured out that if they show people things they like looking at, then they'll stay longer on

their sites. And they'll look at more adverts. So that is exactly what happens. When someone views something online or clicks on a video, these platforms monitor what the person is looking at. And then they search in their massive library of blogs, vlogs, pictures and videos and find something similar to show the person next.

It is called their ALGORITHM. Which is just a fancy way of saying that these platforms rummage around in the back of their cupboard and pull out the thing they know you would most like to see next.

So while it might seem like a coincidence that I clicked on one cute llama picture last week and now I seem to be a big part of the global alpaca appreciation society, I'm not lucky. This was planned.

And the PROBLEM is that if someone shows interest in content that might be untrue, or fake news, the algorithms will show them more and more of that content too.

And this is what happens to people like Carlos. They click on some blogs about climate change being a hoax and then are shown some similar links. They click on those too, so the platform is happy that they are spending loads of time on the website, reading articles and looking at the adverts for new trainers or wireless headphones. But they aren't shown the other side of the debate, because the platform could tell they aren't that interested in reading those blogs. And before they know it, they have made friends with a load of people who all agree that climate change is made up, just like Carlos. And all of this had led to Carlos calling my dad an idiot on Christmas Day from the comfort of the Syed-family's reclining leather sofa.

DON'T BE CARLOS.
BE CAREFUL.

Hmmm . . . I am quite pleased with that slogan. Even if I do say so myself.

But there is a serious message behind my brilliant catchphrase. While you're happily reading blogs, clicking links and watching vlogs, remember that there is usually another side to the story. So take a step back . . . remind yourself that these platforms use an algorithm to show people things they think they'll like and agree with. And just like anything else that might be influencing us, consider whether there might be another point of view or a different opinion. Make sure that what you are seeing really does align with how you think and feel.

ECHO LOCATORS

It is worth remembering that echo chambers can happen in both directions. And they can happen about anything too. If you think that chess is better than tennis and surround yourself with people who think the same, you'll never hear anything about just how fun and healthy tennis club might be. If you think the Prime Minister is rubbish and everyone around you thinks so too, you'll never hear about anything good they've ever done. And surely everyone has done something good, right?

So, how do we know if we are surrounded only by people who think exactly like us? And therefore how do we know we are not seeing both sides of the argument? Carlos had no idea.

Well, it isn't easy to spot whether we have enough information to decide on what we actually think about an issue. After all, we know that it can be nice to be surrounded by people who agree with us. And easy to dismiss anyone who doesn't.

But maybe remembering these rules could help us avoid the echo chamber trap:

1. Remind yourself of how important it is to question your own beliefs and those of others too.
2. Make sure you look for reliable evidence to support your views.
3. Take time to consider whether there is anything you can learn from someone with a different opinion.
4. Don't dismiss someone else's point of view too quickly. It is OK if you hear them out and still don't agree. But give them the time to explain why they have come to their conclusions.

Famous Echo Chambers

Vaccination trepidation (and falsification!)

During the coronavirus pandemic we had to get used to a new normal pretty quickly. We had to make decisions based on information about a virus we had never seen before. We were learning as we went along.

And one of the most inspirational things (I think) to come out of what we learned during that time was the development of the COVID-19 vaccine. It was amazing. Brilliant scientists using their expertise to literally save the world.

Most people were excited by the vaccine. They had looked at the science and could see that it was a way to protect us from the disease and to allow us to go out and about our business rather than having to stay in the house and do school at home.

Some people were more hesitant about the vaccine. They wondered if we needed more time to test it. To look in to the side effects. To make sure it was safe before we jabbed it in to the arms of seven billion people. And it's OK to want to understand all of the facts before you make your decision. There was plenty of information out there to read on the safety of the vaccine.

BUT sadly there was a lot of FAKE NEWS about the vaccine too.

There were wild rumours saying that the whole pandemic was created by Bill Gates (the guy who founded Microsoft, the big tech company). The rumours claimed that he created the super-deadly virus, which has locked down the whole world for two years, JUST so he could then invent a vaccine himself and use it to inject us all with microchips to control our brains.

According to some research in America, 28% of people believed this FAKE NEWS. They genuinely thought that after one dose of the COVID-19 vaccine they'd be chipped up and under the full control of Bill Gates. It wasn't clear what they thought Bill was planning to do once he'd got control . . . turn us all into Microsoft PowerPoint-using zombies?

The story was shared all over social media. And some people fell into an echo chamber, reading and posting more and more reasons why the vaccine was a terrible thing. There were vlogs about how it could alter your DNA. That it might contain sausage (really?). One guy even claimed it had made him crash his car. Even though the smash-up happened three months after he had the jab!

These claims were all false, but they were everywhere. In the UK it is estimated that there are 5.4 million followers of Twitter accounts that contain false vaccine information.

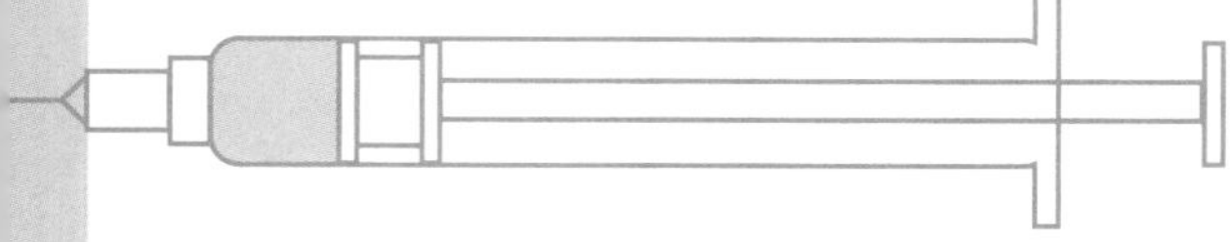

THIS FAKE NEWS WAS HUGE.

And dangerous. Because some people in the echo chamber didn't ever question what they were reading. And they relied on this false information to decide that they wouldn't get vaccinated. They made their decision based on fake news and not on the scientific facts.

CANCEL CULTURE

As Carlos stormed off, he told my dad that he was cancelled. Carlos never wanted to talk to my dad ever again. About anything. So even if Carlos was looking for a new reclining leather sofa, he would NOT be asking my dad (the world expert) for advice on which ones had the best recline. No way. Just because my dad didn't agree with Carlos about climate change, it meant that Carlos was never ever going to speak to him again.

Does that seem a little bit drastic?

Possibly. My dad had a lot to offer. He was from a different culture with different perspectives. He was a professor at a university and had interesting views on politics and what was going on in the world. Even though they disagreed on climate change, maybe Carlos could have learned other things from my dad? And vice versa.

But cancelling people – deciding to totally cut off contact, in person or online, with someone you disagree with – seems to be becoming more and more common.

Now . . . it is a tricky, slippery subject, this cancel culture. Because maybe there are some things that a person might do which would mean it was OK to cancel them. Like, say, if someone stole your watch. You might be justified in deciding never ever to speak to that individual again. And to tell all your friends to do the same. And then phone up their headmaster and see if you can get them expelled from school.

But what if someone said something nasty when they were young and since then has grown up and changed their views? Ollie Robinson is a cricketer who was found to have posted some nasty Tweets ten years ago. They were offensive and hurtful. He said he wasn't proud of it. He apologised and admitted that he had been stupid and his views had changed.

But a lot of people wanted him cancelled and to stop him from ever playing cricket again. The big – and tricky – question with cancel culture is whether one mistake when you are young should ruin your whole life?

In the end, Ollie Robinson didn't lose his whole career (although many people believed he should have). He was banned from playing cricket for several matches and he apologised, telling everyone how 'embarrassed and ashamed' he was of what he had said.

Adele (the mega-famous singer) faced being cancelled too. She went to a party and wore her hair in Bantu knots – a traditional African hairstyle – and posted it on social media. Some people were upset and offended that Adele (a white woman) had dressed up in such a way. Some people got very outraged and even suggested that Adele should 'go to jail with no parole' for this.

We all say or do things that can upset people for lots of reasons. But, should we be allowed to apologise for mistakes we've made? Or should we be cancelled for ever? Should it be OK for people to suggest Adele should go to jail and no one ever listen to her songs ever again?

These are not easy questions to answer. But it is easy to become outraged. Like Carlos. And it is important to consider whether our level of outrage is justified. Did they deserve to be cancelled? To have their whole life, work and reputation ruined? Maybe what they have done is so bad that they should be. Or maybe it is OK for them to apologise and move on, if they understand that they have done something wrong and won't do it again. Or maybe they just hold a different point of view to you, and it is OK to agree to disagree.

Cancel culture is a difficult one to get your head around. So I wonder if it is worth taking a moment to ask: **WHAT DO YOU THINK?** Do you know of anyone (at home, at school or in the news) who has been cancelled? Were they fairly treated? If not, what do you think should have happened differently?

POLAR OPPOSITES

The internet is a wonderful source of information and connection if we use it properly. But all this arguing has shown us how easy it is to find people with some pretty different views about things online too.

People who believe in climate change vs people who think it is a hoax.

People who want the COVID-19 vaccine vs people who don't.

People who love President Donald Trump vs people who think his career peaked with that appearance in *Home Alone 2*.

People who love *Star Wars* vs people who don't even know that Luke and Leia are brother and sister (sorry, did I spoil anything there?).

WHATEVER you think, there will always be someone, somewhere who disagrees with you.

The internet is a wonderful virtual space where everyone can express their opinion. But it is also a place for MASSIVE arguments. And not the good type we talked about in chapter 5. I am on about the hairy-toes-insulting type (remember them? I am trying not to) – where people get out of control and nasty towards others who disagree with them.

And it is all public. Before you know it, what started off as a small tiff is now a mega-row which can be watched by millions of followers online. And it can't ever really be deleted either.

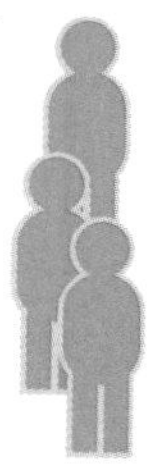

So before you decide to get in to an online argument, ask yourself why you are doing it. If you are genuinely asking for the opinion of someone else, then maybe that is fine. If you are going to say something about hairy toes . . . well . . . maybe have a rethink.

MEGA ALERT:

It is worth remembering that anything you post online (a picture, a video, an insult, a joke) is all there FOR EVER.

For everyone to see. Your mum. Your dad. Your nana. Your teachers. Your children (if you choose to have them in the future). Your girlfriend, boyfriend, future partner. Your future boss in that dream job you've got your eye on.

Once it is out there, you can't stop people copying it and sharing it. So BE CAREFUL about what you post.

IF YOU DON'T WANT YOUR NANA TO SEE IT . . . DO NOT POST IT. EVER.

CHAPTER 7

THE BATTLE OF IDEAS: HOW TO ARGUE AND STAY FRIENDS

SCHOOLED BY SOCRATES

Socrates lived in ancient Greece in the fifth century BCE. And he was one of the greatest teachers of all time. But we don't know this directly from him because he didn't write anything down. Maybe he had lost his pen down the back of his sofa . . . My mum once found twenty-four pens (and a harmonica) down the back of our sofa when my dad's reclining mechanism broke down one Sunday morning. There was a Bic Biro caught in it, and it was mayhem. There was green ink everywhere and my brother attempted to play the national anthem on the harmonica while my mum tried to fix the mechanism.

Anyway, it is unlikely that Socrates had lost his pen. He hated writing. You see, he was not what we would call an 'early adopter' of technology. He wasn't racing out to embrace the latest inventions that the world of ancient Greece had to offer. The sick high-tech item back then was . . . wait for it . . . the BOOK. But he thought this technology was a disaster. He thought that writing stuff down was a bad idea. That it would mean you would put quill to parchment and then immediately forget all of your thoughts once they were written down. So he didn't do it.

Instead, his students (such as Plato, another very famous ancient Greek philosopher) wrote things down. They noted their memories of him and the conversations they had together. Not ideal, as they described him as a seriously ugly dude with a snub nose and bulging eyes. But if you are going to refuse to embrace the technology and won't write anything down, then you take the risk of being described for the rest of history as looking like a scrunched-up frog.

Socrates didn't care about his appearance, though. Which was unusual back in ancient Athens. The ancient Greeks thought that being beautiful was very important.

He was interested in learning. In understanding the world. In ideas. And he believed that the best way to understand the truth was to discuss and disagree so you could work out who was right.

He would debate with the intellectuals of Athens, Greece, in the town square. Gently questioning them about their beliefs and why they held them.

And guess what . . . quite often, this questioning would reveal that their beliefs were not based on very much at all. But Socrates was not out to make his fellow Athenians look stupid. He wasn't aggressive or confrontational. He was just out to show that we often hold views and opinions that we can't back up with evidence.

And this was a new method of learning in Athens back then. Until Socrates turned up, the Greeks believed that you should try and persuade someone to *agree* with *your* view. And if you couldn't manage to do that then you had lost. It was a combat. A verbal fight with a winner and a loser.

But Socrates was different. He realised (like we have through this book) that we can't know everything ourselves. And by understanding what other people think and believe, we can make ourselves smarter.

So, if we can get good at debating and questioning, like Socrates; if we can steal some of his tips and tricks to help us (slow) think and analyse things, then we are going to be more confident in our opinions and in expressing our thoughts to others.

It is called critical thinking. And this is a seriously good skill to have. So . . . Socrates . . . let's get into this.

HOW DO YOU HAVE AN EFFECTIVE ARGUMENT?

FIRST: Think critically

Did you know . . . Researchers from Cornell University (great university in America) asked people whether they could explain how a zip worked. Almost everybody was very confident that they could. After all, most people use zips every day.

DO YOU KNOW HOW THEY WORK?

You do? Right . . . Go on then. Have a go at explaining just how those little metal teeth keep your coat closed. Hmmmmm . . . harder than it sounds, huh? And that is what the researchers found. While everyone BELIEVED they knew exactly how a zip worked, when questioned on it, they had no idea.

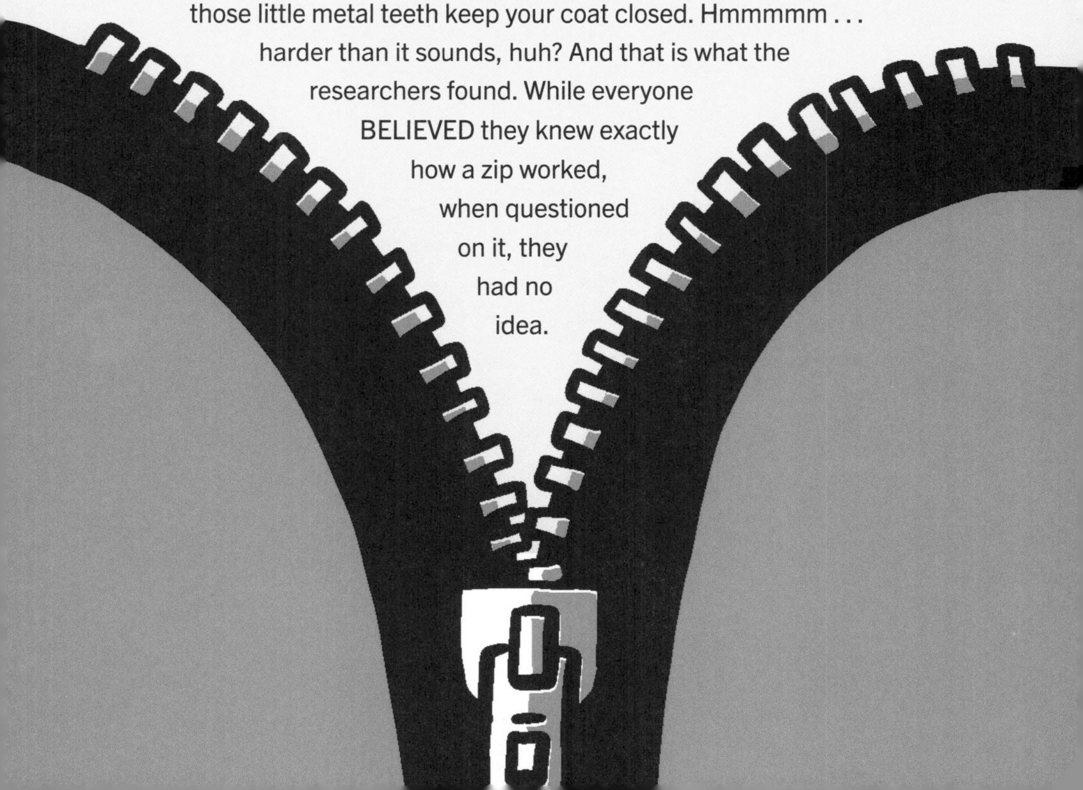

We have a tendency to think we understand things when we have absolutely no clue at all!

So, to make sure that we understand what we believe in, we need to take the time to investigate, look at the evidence and learn what our opinions are based on by using what I call our Critical Thinking Toolkit.

If you do this before you get into a discussion or debate, then you'll be as sure as you can be that you believe in and understand your point of view.

There's some easy steps to remember:

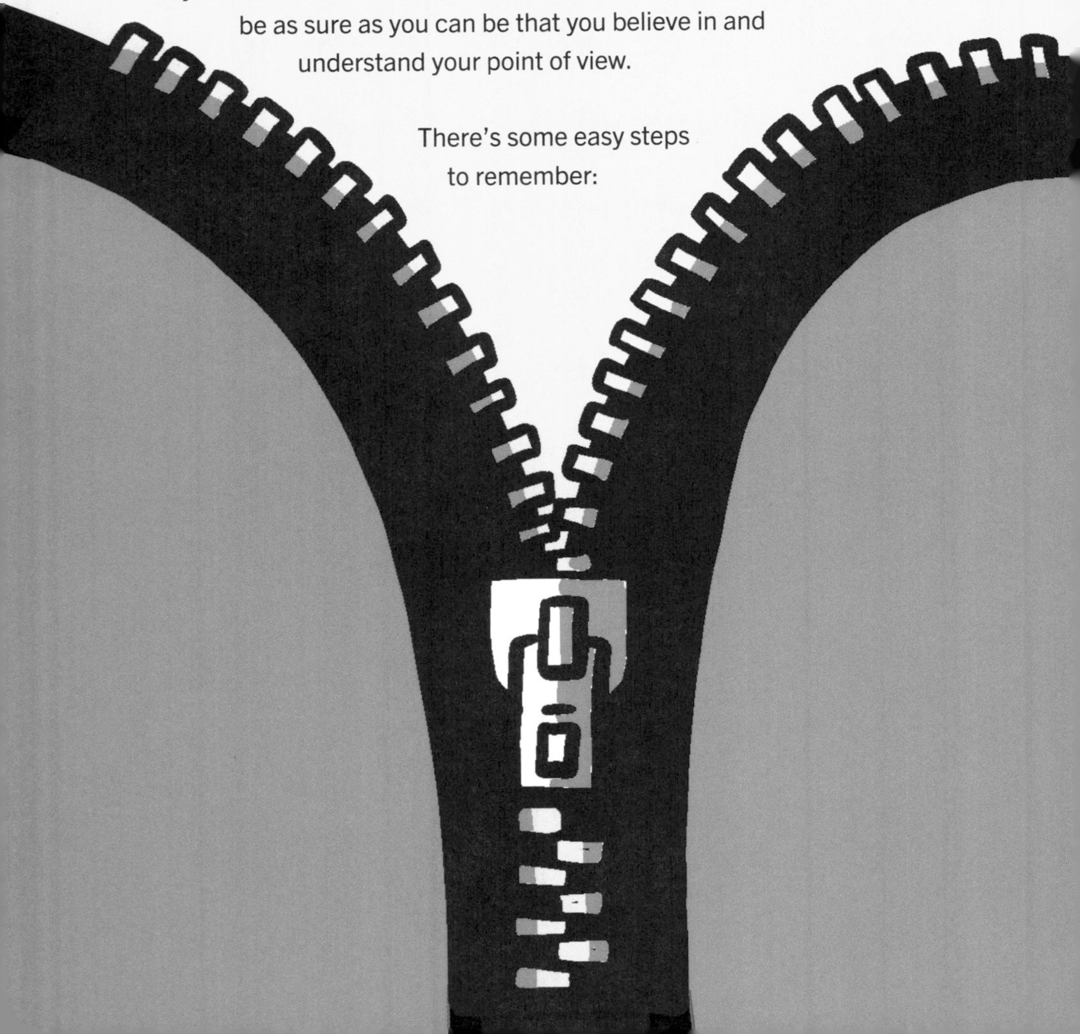

1. **What's the problem you're solving?** What is the question you want to ask? Or what is the issue you want to discuss?

2. **What's your evidence?** Have you done your research? What questions have you asked to understand the issue better? Have you looked at the facts from reliable books or websites?

3. **What are your influences?** Have you jumped to any conclusions? What anchors are swaying your opinions?

4. **What's the opposite point of view to yours?** Have you considered what the other person or group is thinking? Why would they believe that?

5. **What's your solution?** How are you going to present your views? What is the best way to make your point without getting into a hairy-toes-insult situation?

Let's take an example.

Your school has decided that they want your class to do an extra maths lesson. ON A SATURDAY MORNING.

NIGHTMARE.

We might be tempted to scream and shout, 'Are you *TRYING* to ruin my life? I hate this school.' But this is our Fast Thinking kicking in, and I suspect that this is not going to get us very far.

So let's use our Slow Thinking and see whether our new Critical Thinking Toolkit could be helpful in getting our Saturday lie-in back. Maybe we can present the school with some thoughtful alternatives . . .

Now, I know I wasn't *actually* at school during the pandemic (are you saying I'm old?!) but . . . imagine I was. I might have thought . . .

What's the problem?

I'm already busy enough. There is already a tonne of extra work from school. Then there's tennis practice and chores at home. At this rate there'll be no time for sleeping or eating. I'll be doing geometry in the bath if they get their way.

What's the evidence?

Well, come to think of it, we did fall behind with maths during the pandemic. So maybe we do need some extra help. But some people fell further behind than others. I mean, Marcus Hawkins came back thinking a protractor was a fancy farmyard vehicle.

But I had worked pretty hard during home-schooling. I hadn't missed a lesson. And while I wasn't the best with a Venn diagram, I was pretty good at most topics. I definitely wasn't the worst in the class.

So . . . I want to ask school some questions before they haul us all in every weekend. Questions like: How have you decided who needs help? And how can you tell what topics they need help with?

What are my influences?

Apart from the fact that I might miss the famous Syed Saturday sausage sandwich for breakfast if I have to go to school, I don't see why we need extra school. We go every day. And Jacinta Insley said that we already go to school more often than any other kids in the world.

It felt that way to me. But I did wonder if that was actually true. It turns out that Jacinta was spreading a bit of fake news. When I looked in to it, we go for 190 days per year. And kids in China go for 220 days. That is a whole extra month. Which means that a whole lot more fractions and equations are happening in Beijing than in Berkshire.

So maybe a few extra hours of maths is not quite as harsh as I first thought.

What's the opposite point of view?

That we have fallen behind in the pandemic. And maths is a very important life skill. And if the teachers are willing to give up their time on a Saturday to help us, we should take this up gratefully.

Hmmmm . . . they might have a point.

What's my solution?

Taking everything in to account – as well as the fact that Mary Suarez was asked to draw a pie chart and handed something in with sketches of a pastry-crusted steak and kidney on it – maybe we do need help. But how about a test to see exactly what each person needs to work on?

Then the school could run sessions focused on particular topics. So not everybody would have to go to every extra class. You could just go to the ones you need to.

That way, there would be fewer people in each session and everyone would get more attention.

Oh, and could we do it on a Tuesday after school rather than a Saturday? I really don't want to miss the Saturday sausage sandwich.

NEXT: Set the rules

Before you start, think about how you want to finish the conversation. And I can guarantee that it isn't wrestling around and shouting about toe hair.

Decide to keep calm. Don't raise your voice. Suggest that you want to 'discuss' or 'debate' an issue rather than get confrontational about it. In a court of law, barristers will address each other as 'My Learned Friend' even while they are having huge arguments over the case that they're disagreeing about. That way of addressing their opponent reminds them that everyone is entitled to speak their mind and to be respectful of that.

ALWAYS: Listen

You've been there, right? Arguing about who sits in the front seat of the car. Before you know it, everyone is screaming at the same time. No one can hear anything.

If you are too busy shouting your point of view and speaking over everyone else to make yourself heard, then you might miss out on learning something. Socrates was clear that he wanted to listen and understand why people felt strongly about issues. That way he might learn something he didn't already know or see where their logic was wrong.

Maybe your sister has hurt her leg and needs the extra leg room in the front seat. Maybe your brother needs to be up there to help with the directions to his judo lesson. Maybe your cousin gets super car-sick and might vomit all over you if he is in the back.

You won't know any of this if you are part of the screaming competition.

Listening helps to show others that you are interested in what they have to say and are taking them seriously. It makes them feel like you are open to ideas and value their experiences. And it helps you to see a different perspective which you could learn from.

Listening makes for a much more productive discussion.

MAKE SURE TO: Build Goodwill

Have you ever been to the Difficult Conversations Laboratory? And I'm not talking about my brother's bedroom. This is an actual place, in a proper university, in New York. I promise you this is not fake news. It's where real people go to have a row while scientists study the arguments and debates between them.

And guess what they have found . . . it won't surprise you . . . but the best conversations happen when people are willing to listen and learn. Yeah, yeah, I know, we already know that.

But what is interesting is what they have observed about conversations that DON'T end well. There is a pattern. The people arguing will get to a point, just like my brother and I do, when they will stop listening and get stuck. They will get negative and start thinking that everything the other person says is stupid or plain wrong. Then they can get insulting and personal.

So – the big question is – what's the difference between a good row and one that goes off the rails?

The scientists in New York think there is a fairly simple answer. In the more reasonable debates, the people spend a bit of time building some goodwill. Trying to reduce confrontation by being a little bit nicer to each other.

Think of it this way: You want to ask your dad for more pocket money. When he says no, you can go one of two ways . . .

Option 1 – Shout at him. Is he serious? Does he really think you can live off £4 a week? Does he not care that you will be the only one at school with so little money? Is he bothered that he is ruining your life? Before telling him you hate him and storming off upstairs.

OR

Option 2 – You can build some goodwill. Instead of shouting, saying 'I understand that money is tight' shows that you get where he is coming from. Offer to help him out: 'I could do some chores to earn a bit extra.' Or say, 'I'd like to be a bit more independent with my money and start saving for things.'

Which do you think is going to get you the new pair of trainers you've been hoping for?

FIND TIME TO: Practise

Being able to discuss and debate well is a super skill to have. Not only will it help you to argue for the things you believe in, it will make you smarter and more knowledgeable too.

And now we've got the tools to do it.

But we've got to get out there and speak up. Because the more we practise, the better we will get at it.

So have a go at persuading your sister to lend you her favourite pair of jeans. Talk to your mum about her thoughts on climate change. Ask your teacher about what they think of lowering the voting age to sixteen.

Join the school debating society if there is one. And if there isn't, maybe try and persuade the school to start one?

Listen. Learn. And don't forget to Speak Up.

CONCLUSION

DON'T BE AFRAID TO CHANGE YOUR MIND

DILYS,

my dad was shouting to my mum from the sitting room one evening when he got back from work.

YEEEEEESSSSS,

came my mum's quiet reply. She knew what was coming.

WHY IS THERE A NEW BRICK WALL IN HERE?

and

WHERE EXACTLY IS MY SOFA?

This kind of conversation happened weekly in our house.

My mum loves a room makeover more than Kim Kardashian loves a camera.

So, regularly, my dad would leave the house and by the time he returned there would be some major change to the decor. And I don't mean a lick of paint or a new lamp. I mean the whole shebang. Carpets changed, walls moved, windows added. We'd come home from school and think we had gone to the wrong house.

One day she painted the back of the house a kind of acid yellow colour. She said it made her feel cheerful; Barry from next door said it made him feel queasy. He wouldn't go out into his garden without sunglasses, even at night. And the time she accidentally bricked up the bathroom trying to create two en suites was a tense night. She couldn't get Dave the builder back until the next day, and my dad had to shower with the hose in the back garden. Barry had his sunglasses on that night as well.

You see, my dad was a man of habit (I mean, he'd only ever had one style of reclining sofa). My mum thought he'd never agree to her new decoration ideas, so she'd do it all while he was out and surprise him. But one time she went a step too far. I mean, it was impressive what she had managed to achieve between 8 a.m. and 6 p.m. But my dad couldn't seem to see that. She'd blocked off the dining room from the sitting room to create something she was describing as a 'sun room with essence of Venice'. She'd painted a gondola on the wall and was sitting (on the reclining sofa) with her feet in the paddling pool she'd filled up and put on the floor.

I FEEL LIKE I AM IN THE PIAZZA SAN MARCO, IN THE MIDDLE OF VENICE,

she said as my dad came into the room with a furious look on his face.

BUT IT IS AS SMALL AS A SHOEBOX. WE CAN'T EVEN FIT THE TV IN HERE WITH ALL OF THE SOFAS,

he pointed out.

He wasn't wrong.

And this is the thing with my mum – when she is faced with this evidence, she doesn't mind admitting that she might have made a mistake.

We enjoyed it that night, had pizza and gelato (well, they were Mini Milks) with our feet in the paddling pool and my mum sang some Italian opera she had heard on Classic FM. But, by 6 p.m. the next night, there was no sun room, no sign of Venice and the sofas were back in front of the TV.

I had to admire my mum. Not just because she could basically build a whole house in less than twenty-four hours. But because she was and is totally open-minded. If someone has a different view and she thinks they might be right, she has no problem adapting what she thinks. She doesn't get angry or frustrated like a lot of people do when they are told they might be wrong. She listens, thinks about it and decides whether she might need to change her mind.

And this is not easy.

But one of the final things that I want to leave you with (I know, it's sad, but we are getting to the end of the book) is one of the most important . . .

. . . that it really is OK to change your mind. And don't ever feel like you can't.

THINK LIKE A SCIENTIST

People have a tendency to get defensive and annoyed if they are told they are wrong. To dig their heals in. And even start shouting about hairy toes.

It can be really hard to change your mind. People get embarrassed that they have believed in things that are wrong (remember those who believed Planet Nibiru was going to smash the earth to pieces?). They feel the pressure to defend themselves so they don't seem stupid.

But the only foolish thing is holding on to opinions that are not right or that you don't believe in any more.

Imagine if people hadn't changed our minds about some of the things we used to believe? Women still wouldn't be able to vote. Married women wouldn't be allowed to work. Being gay would still be illegal. And the Syed family would still have those onions all over the house (remember those?).

So try and think like a scientist because they have no problem changing their minds if they need to. Scientists spend their whole lives doing experiments to test their ideas. And if they don't work then they realise they have to have a rethink and try something new. That is how science works. It questions what we think we know, tests theories and adapts in order to find the truth. In other words: scientists aren't afraid to be wrong and we shouldn't be either.

So if you have changed your mind and think that Ed Sheeran's new song is quite good, after you'd told everyone who'd listen that you thought his other ones were rubbish, that's OK. Or if you've been saying for years that you want to be a doctor when you're older but now you'd rather be a chef, that's OK too. We're all learning all the time. About the world around us, about other people and most importantly about ourselves. It can be hard to admit that we have changed our mind. Especially if we have told everyone (loudly and often) what we used to think. But it is much worse to stick with an idea or opinion we don't believe in any more.

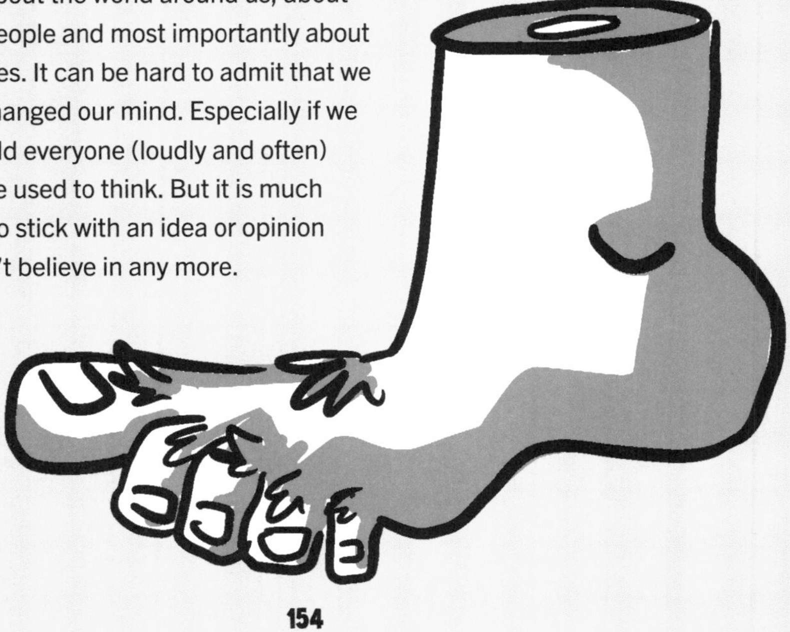

GO AND HAVE A THINK . . .

We've covered a lot in this book and met a whole crowd of people who helped me to understand how we think, what can influence us and how we can make our own decisions. I'm sure you've got a crowd who influence you and get you thinking too.

Mr Phelan – the jumper, who showed us the dangers of jumping to conclusions. The difference between Fast and Slow Thinking. And why we can form thoughts and opinions that don't always reflect what we think and feel.

My dad – who showed us many things. How to skip with no rope. The benefits of a reclining leather sofa. But more importantly, how easily we can be influenced and why it is important to consider a different point of view.

My brother – let's not give him too much credit. After all, he did say I had hairy toes. And he eats Bombay Bad Boy pot noodles in bed. But he got caught up in some fake news (and thought he'd eaten a tarantula) and showed us how easy it is to believe things that might not be quite right.

Jack Harvey – who showed us that our background and our experiences can shape the way we see situations. We need to expect that other people won't think exactly like us.

Anders Mortenson – well . . . just say hi to him if you are ever in a cemetery in Copenhagen . . . He'll be there . . . having a party.

Carlos – where do I even start . . .? Take some raisins if you are going to settle in for a climate change debate with this guy. But recognise that we are all capable of falling into an echo chamber which can mean we don't ever see the other side of the argument.

Socrates – I'm not sure how he would feel about being included in this list of characters. But . . . he is now an old (very old, like 2,500 years old) friend of ours. And he was a brilliantly skilled debater. And that is a skill we want to have. To be able to question and understand the views of others. Calmly and with the belief that we might learn something from their point of view.

My mum – if you want a rainbow painting across your bedroom, let me know. She could probably do it for you tomorrow between 3.30 p.m. and 5 p.m. But even if you change your mind, she won't mind. She's happy to admit it if she doesn't get things quite right. And so should we. Let's not hold on to ideas that we no longer believe in. Be confident to change your view.

And now, it is over to you. To use all of the tools and tips we have learned, to go out there and make your voice heard in the right way. I promise you, you are worth hearing. Be confident and speak up.

So,

WHAT DO YOU THINK?

Because I, for one, am very interested to hear.

DISCOVER MORE AWESOME . . .

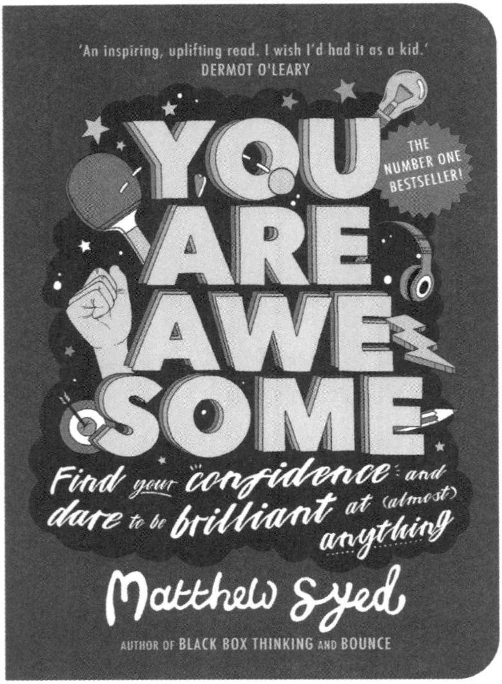

Paperback | 978 1 5263 6115 8
E-book | 978 1 5263 6133 2
Audio book | 978 1 5263 6157 8

YOU ARE AWESOME

"I'm no good at sport . . . " "I can't do maths . . . " Sound familiar? If you believe you can't do something, chances are you won't try. But what if you really could get better at maths or sport? What if you could excel at anything you put your mind to? This inspiring guide empowers young readers to find the confidence to realise their potential with a positive growth mindset.

BOOKS BY MATTHEW SYED!

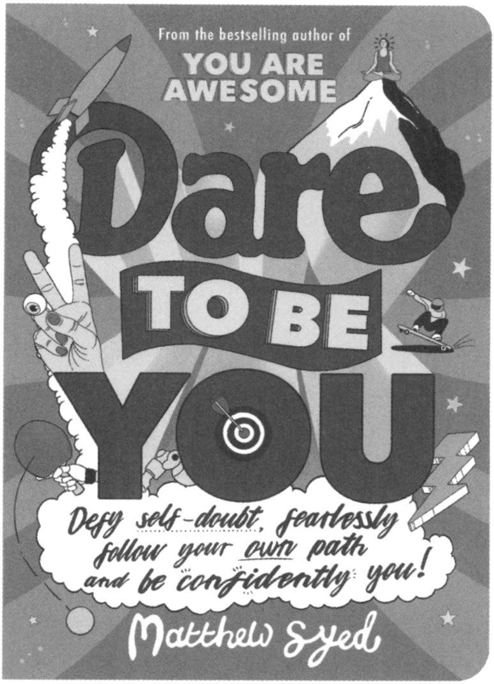
From the bestselling author of
YOU ARE AWESOME
Dare
TO BE
YOU
Defy self-doubt, fearlessly follow your own path and be confidently you!
Matthew Syed

Paperback | 978 1 5263 6237 7
E-book | 978 1 5263 6238 4
Audio book | 978 1 5263 6239 1

DARE TO BE YOU

What would you dare to try if you stopped worrying about fitting in? If you're the kind of person who thinks: I don't like standing out from the crowd . . . I wish I could be more like the cool kids . . . There's no point trying to change things . . . then this book is for you. Because guess what? There's no such thing as normal.

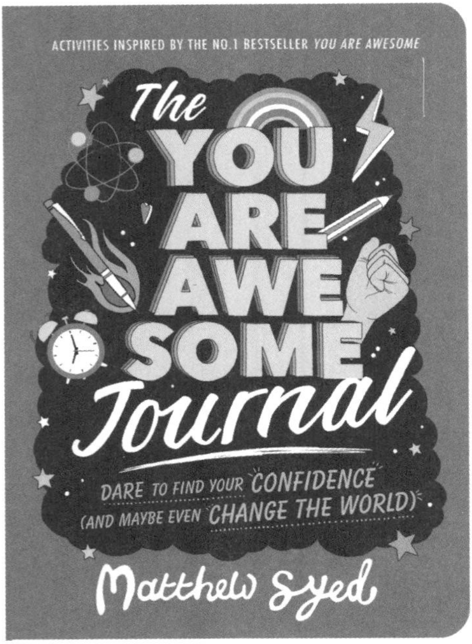

Paperback | 978 1 5263 6166 0

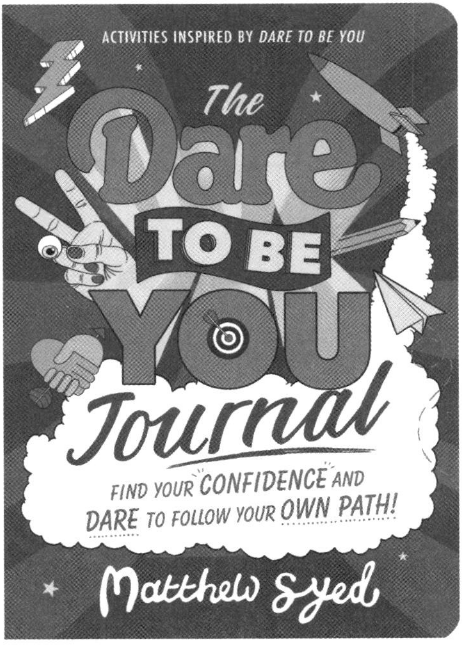

Paperback | 978 1 5263 6314 5